cookies
for kids' cancer
BEST BAKE SALE COOKBOOK

cookies™
for kids' cancer
cookiesforkidscancer.org

Gretchen Holt-Witt

with Sally Sampson

Photography by Lucy Schaeffer

cookies
for kids' cancer

BEST BAKE SALE COOKBOOK

WILEY

John Wiley & Sons, Inc.

Photography Copyright © 2011 by Lucy Schaeffer

Designed by Cassandra J. Pappas

Food styling by Cyd McDowell

Prop styling by Michelle Rotman

Published by John Wiley & Sons, Inc., Hoboken, New Jersey

Published simultaneously in Canada

For general information on our other products and services or for technical support, please contact our Customer Care Department within the United States at (800) 762-2974, outside the United States at (317) 572-3993 or fax (317) 572-4002.

Wiley also publishes its books in a variety of electronic formats. Some content that appears in print may not be available in electronic books. For more information about Wiley products, visit our web site at www.wiley.com.

Library of Congress Cataloging-in-Publication Data

Witt, Gretchen Holt, 1967–
  Cookies for kids' cancer : bake sale cookbook / Gretchen Holt-Witt ; with Sally Sampson ; Photography by Lucy Schaeffer.
    p. cm.
  Includes bibliographical references and index.
  ISBN 978-0-470-94761-6 (cloth : alk. paper); 978-1-118-11053-9 (ebk); 978-1-118-11054-6 (ebk); 978-1-118-11055-3 (ebk)
  1. Cookies. 2. Cookbooks. I. Sampson, Sally, 1955–II. Title.
  TX772.W5485 2011
  641.8'654—dc22   2010048202

Printed in China

10 9 8 7 6 5 4 3 2 1

To Prince Liam

ે

Our love, our life, our inspiration,
and number one Good Cookie.
We love you.

—Mommy, Daddy, and Ella

contents

introduction

It was never my goal in life to be known as the mom daring enough (or is it crazy enough?) to bake and sell 96,000 cookies for a good cause when, in truth, I had absolutely no idea what I was doing. And I certainly never dreamed of starting a pediatric cancer nonprofit that encourages people to host bake sales as a way to raise money to support research. Honestly, I wasn't even much of a baker.

Now don't get me wrong, I love to bake. And even more than baking, I love sharing beautiful and delicious cookies, cupcakes, breads, bars, and even elaborately decorated cakes. To me, the act of baking is an act of love, and while I am passionate about baking, my true passion is being Liam's and Ella's Mommy.

But my goals in life changed in an instant when my precious 2½-year-old son was diagnosed with pediatric cancer in 2007, and suddenly only one thing in the world mattered to me, to my husband, and to his adoring sister Ella: Liam's health. Suddenly, I found myself asking a million questions related to pediatric cancer—about treatment options, side effects, long-term ramifications, and worst of all, why I didn't know more about the disease

I was just learning claims the lives of more children in the U.S. than any other. These are not questions any parent should have to ask, and the answers we learned left a few things crystal clear.

First, we learned there are not nearly enough treatment options currently available for kids battling cancer. And of the options available, many of the drugs will likely cause harm equal to or greater than the cancer itself or, even worse, were not even designed for use on kids, so the dosing or long-term side effects are just now known.

Second, we learned of doctors and researchers across the country and around the world committing countless hours and years to the discovery of new and improved treatments for kids with cancer. These doctors are dedicating their careers to saving kids' lives, which makes them heroes to all who know them.

Finally, the most crushing immediate lesson we learned is that these hardworking and dedicated doctors and researchers often place their ideas on a shelf due to lack of funding to begin clinical

trials. New treatments are largely dependent upon private funding. And testing theories, medicines, and treatments in clinical studies is how science moves forward. There's only one problem: In many cases they don't have the funding needed to develop therapies that have been proven to work in a lab, and drug companies are not interested in making them because they're just not profitable enough. So essentially, there is a need to find private funding from people like you and me, who share a passion for children and who want to help doctors create new treatments for the battle against pediatric cancer. But since, as one doctor told us, "kids with cancer don't make headlines," getting the word out to people about the need and inspiring them to get involved is often an uphill battle. And as one TV producer told me, she didn't want to cover a story about pediatric cancer because it just wasn't "happy."

With those three simple lessons in mind, my family first set out to reclaim Liam's body from the cancer that was trying to

claim him. Chemotherapy, radiation, a nearly 12-hour surgery, and antibody therapy were the first lines of defense that together helped us get him to a stable place by the fall of 2007, when our thoughts quickly turned to our second line of defense— supporting the doctors and researchers who desperately need funds to introduce more clinical trials that offer children more options and families hope.

The holidays were fast approaching, and like many, my thoughts turned to sugary, crispy, crunchy, delicious, and irresistible baked treats that so many enjoy that time of year. But in a moment nearly as life changing as learning my child had cancer, I suddenly saw baked goods as more than just another way to spend time with my kids, create memories, and show them my complete adoration. Suddenly, I saw baked goods as the essential ingredients that would inspire others to join the fight against pediatric cancer. In the blink of an eye, I went from seeing chocolate chip cookies as treats to seeing them as the fuel to drive science into the future. And then I did some math . . .

Eighty (the number of families we knew at the time who had children battling the same cancer as Liam), multiplied times 100 (the number of dozens of cookies I hoped each family would be able to encourage family or friends to purchase) = 8,000 dozen cookies . . . or 96,000 cookies. But seriously, could I, a full-time working mother of a young child and toddler who happened to be in active cancer treatment bake that many cookies to raise funds for a new treatment for pediatric cancer research? I knew I didn't have a choice. It had to happen.

My next phone call was to my good friend Sally Sampson, recipe writer extraordinaire who also happens to bake Liam's favorite cookies of all time, citrus shortbread. I knew her expertise would guide an answer to the burning question of whether I could do this, or was I being overly ambitious? Without hesitation Sally said yes, I could most definitely bake that many cookies. And so then my wheels really started turning . . . and with every turn the signs pointed to cookies as being the sweet answer to our stubborn problem of how to innocently get people involved in pediatric cancer research.

We needed recipes. Done, thanks to Sally, who instantly opened up her vault of recipes to find the perfect ones for large-scale baking. We needed supplies. Done, thanks to the support of one unstoppable volunteer at a supply company who never quit until we had the perfect packaging for our treats. We needed a commercial kitchen with the right certification to bake our cookies. Oh my, I never could have anticipated how much of a challenge that would be in New York City. I could write a separate book on the ovens from that kitchen. Let's just say, we never let the kitchen challenges stand in the way of our desire to bake cookies.

Then we needed volunteers. And this is where the magic kicked in. More than 250 people—not just my friends, but friends of friends who heard about the idea and simply insisted on helping—showed up for seventeen consecutive days, staying late into the night and sometimes early into the morning hours to bake, cool, package, and ship all 8,000 dozen cookies that sold in a matter of days, thanks to the support of fellow cancer families who spread the word and to the news media who proved that, in fact, the need for funding pediatric cancer research is news-worthy and not always a "downer" story.

Our little online business that didn't have one cus-tomer on the day we opened, nor any reputation to rely on, sold to people all across the country. We worked and worked and worked to raise more than $400,000 for a promising new treatment for pediatric cancer. Then we turned off the ovens only to learn we had ignited a fire within hundreds of people across the country.

People who love cookies loved the idea of sending cookies that support kids battling cancer as gifts.

People who love their families loved being able to send cookies to other families as a way to say "I love you."

And most importantly, people who love to bake felt inspired . . . to bake from their own community and do what they could to help.

We spent months asking ourselves how we could make it work, to create from scratch a national nonprofit organization led by a grassroots call to action for individuals to bake as a way to join the fight against pediatric cancer. What would our priorities be? What would our message be? How could we create an organization that would inspire more than just bakers, more than just moms? We wanted to inspire anyone, everyone in the same way our brave son had inspired us.

And so, though it was never my goal in life to be a mom on a mission, I learned to embrace the idea that bake sales really could change the world. Our logo was a universally loved image of a cookie with the message "Let's make the letter 'C' stand for cookies." With my belief in a better future for my son and all children battling cancer, and those who have yet to be called into battle, Cookies for Kids' Cancer was born in September 2008. Our mission of raising awareness and funds for pediatric cancer research through bake sales inspires others to change the world of pediatric cancer one bake sale at a time. And thousands of bake sales later, we stand witness to the power of individual cookies.

Cookies are funding new treatments for pediatric cancer. Cookies inspire individuals to fire up their ovens to host an event. Cookies are essential at huge events where tens of thousands of dollars are raised in what feels like a matter of minutes. Cookies are just as important at smaller events featuring homemade signs held by sticky little fingers, asking friends

and neighbors to drop in some change for new treatments for pediatric cancer. Cookies are at schools and churches and festivals, offering donors a sweet memory of what is otherwise an unsavory subject. And with that sweetness comes a love of baking and children and togetherness and hope for a better tomorrow. I'm guessing it is one of those loves—baking, children, or hope—that drew you to the pages of this book. And for that, I am grateful. I hope all of Sally Sampson's incredible recipes inspire you to hone your baking skills and in turn wow your bake sale crowd. I hope our tips from hosts will make planning a bake sale easier and simpler and less stressful. And I believe the words from hosts across the country will ignite in you the fire to change the world, one cookie at a time.

chocolate chip

cookies

the cookie that started it all: chocolate chip oatmeal cookies

YIELD: **3** TO **4** DOZEN COOKIES

Chocolate chip cookies are universal favorites at bake sales, but this recipe was developed specifically for Cookies for Kids' Cancer first bake sale—the 96,000-cookie one. No matter the season, these dense, buttery, yet light cookies—thanks to the oats—sell more than any other.

Use the best-quality chocolate chips you can find. Don't bother making these cookies if you are scrimping on chips!

2 sticks (½ pound) unsalted butter, at room temperature

1 cup light brown sugar

½ cup granulated sugar

1 large egg, at room temperature

1 large egg yolk, at room temperature

1 tablespoon vanilla extract

2 cups all-purpose flour

1 cup quick-cooking or old-fashioned rolled oats

1 teaspoon baking powder

1 teaspoon baking soda

1 teaspoon kosher salt

3 cups semi-sweet chocolate chips

- Preheat the oven to 325°F. Line a cookie sheet with parchment paper.

- Place the butter and sugars in the bowl of a mixer fitted with a paddle and beat until smooth and creamy. Add the egg, egg yolk, and vanilla, one at a time, beating well between additions.

- Place the flour, oats, baking powder, baking soda, and salt in a separate bowl; mix well and add to the butter mixture. Beat until everything is well incorporated. Scrape down the sides of the bowl, add the chocolate chips, and beat again.

- Form the dough into heaping-teaspoon-size balls and place them about 2 inches apart on the prepared cookie sheet. Using your palm, gently press down. Alternatively, you can roll the dough into a log (see next page).

• Transfer to the oven and bake until the cookies begin to brown at the edges, 12 to 15 minutes. Cool on the cookie sheet. Transfer to a wire rack and repeat with the remaining dough.

how to make cookie logs ೪೨

To prepare cookie logs, roll the dough into 1- to 2-inch cylinders, depending upon the cookie, and cover with parchment paper. Place the cylinders in a resealable plastic bag. Refrigerate until slightly firm, about 20 minutes, and then re-form the cylinder to ensure that the shape is uniform. Return to the refrigerator until the dough is firm, at least 1 hour and up to 5 days. When ready to bake, slice the cylinder into rounds ⅛ to ½ inch thick, depending upon the cookie. If desired, freeze the dough for up to 1 month.

BAKE SALE TIPS ೪೨ *from laura black*

• Moving billboards—Our team of volunteers got together a week before the big day to decorate our car windows with details about the bake sale. Using window paint, we wrote the date, time, and location of the event and drew pictures of cookies all over the side and rearview mirrors. People all over town learned about the bake sale thanks to our cars that served as billboards.
• Kids playing dress-up—We created simple-to-make cookie and cupcake costumes for kids to wear during the event. Kids at bake sales are cute, but kids dressed up like treats are irresistible.
• Make it local—Our inspiration was several local families with children fighting pediatric cancer. By having an "inspiration table" with pictures and stories from area kids fighting cancer, we made sure everyone who stopped by understood that kids in our town are impacted by pediatric cancer in the hopes of inspiring everyone to give generously.

oatmeal raisin cranberry cookies

Oatmeal Raisin Cranberry Cookies are a favorite at morning bake sales. Offer them alongside muffins and breads for a special morning indulgence.

2 sticks (½ pound) unsalted butter, at room temperature

1 cup dark brown sugar

½ cup granulated sugar

2 large eggs, at room temperature

1 tablespoon vanilla extract

1 tablespoon water

2½ cups quick-cooking or old-fashioned rolled oats

1¾ cups all-purpose flour

1 teaspoon baking soda

1 teaspoon ground cinnamon

½ teaspoon kosher salt

¾ cup raisins or currants

¾ cup dried cranberries

- Preheat the oven to 375°F. Line a cookie sheet with parchment paper.
- Place the butter and sugars in the bowl of a mixer fitted with a paddle and beat until smooth and creamy. Add the eggs, vanilla, and water, one at a time, beating well between additions. Place the oats, flour, baking soda, cinnamon, and salt in a separate bowl, mix well, and add to the butter mixture. Beat until everything is well incorporated. Scrape down the sides of the bowl, add the raisins and cranberries and beat until just combined. Scrape down the sides of the bowl and beat again.
- Form the dough into heaping-teaspoon-size balls and place them about 2 inches apart on the prepared cookie sheet. Using your palm, gently press down. Alternatively, you can roll the dough into a log (see facing page).
- Transfer to the oven and bake until the cookies begin to brown at the edges, 12 to 15 minutes. Cool on the cookie sheet. Transfer to a wire rack and repeat with the remaining dough.

toasted coconut shortbread

YIELD: ABOUT 3 DOZEN COOKIES ❧

W e've noticed that most people have a love/hate relationship with coconut (we haven't found anyone who is neutral), but don't let that stop you from offering coconut cookies at a bake sale. Just be sure you celebrate the coconut you offer—make a special sign for your Toasted Coconut Shortbread, include a cute illustration, and encourage samples. Coconut lovers will love you for the special treat.

½ cup sweetened flaked coconut

2 sticks (½ pound) unsalted butter, at room temperature

¼ cup confectioners' sugar

¼ cup granulated sugar

2¼ cups all-purpose flour

¼ teaspoon kosher salt

- Preheat the oven to 250°F.

- Spread the coconut evenly on a cookie sheet, transfer to the oven, and bake until just golden, about 10 minutes. Set aside to cool.

- Place the butter, coconut, and sugars in the bowl of a mixer fitted with a paddle and beat until smooth and creamy. Scrape down the sides of the bowl, add the flour and salt, beat well, and scrape again. Form the dough into a 1½-inch-diameter log and cover with parchment paper. Place the log in a resealable plastic bag and refrigerate at least 1 hour and up to 2 days, or freeze up to 2 months.

- Preheat the oven to 325°F. Line a cookie sheet with parchment paper.

- With the tip of a very sharp knife, cut ¼- to ½-inch slices of the dough and place 2 inches apart on the prepared cookie sheet. Transfer to the oven and bake until the cookies are just beginning to brown on the edges, about 20 minutes. Transfer to a wire rack to cool. Let the cookie sheet cool completely between batches and repeat with the remaining dough.

classic sugar cookies

YIELD: 3 TO 4 DOZEN COOKIES ᘒ≈

D on't even think about having a bake sale without these classic must-have cookies!

2 sticks (½ pound) unsalted butter, at room temperature	1 large egg yolk, at room temperature
1 cup granulated sugar, plus additional for sprinkling	1 teaspoon vanilla extract
1 large egg, at room temperature	2½ cups all-purpose flour
	1 teaspoon baking powder
	½ teaspoon kosher salt

- Place the butter and sugar in the bowl of a mixer fitted with a paddle and beat until the mixture is smooth and creamy. Add the egg and egg yolk, one at a time, beating well between additions. Place the flour, baking powder, and salt in a separate bowl, mix well, and add to the butter mixture. Beat until everything is well incorporated. Scrape down the sides of the bowl and form the dough into two balls. Place each ball into the center of a large resealable plastic bag. Place each bag on the counter and, using a rolling pin, roll the dough from the center toward the edges until it is between ⅛ and ¼ inch thick. Refrigerate at least 1 hour and up to 2 days. Alternatively, you can form the dough into a 1-inch log (page 4).

- Preheat the oven to 375°F. Remove 1 sheet of dough from the refrigerator at a time.

- Using any shape cookie cutter, punch out cookies and place 2 inches apart on an unbuttered cookie sheet. Transfer to the oven and bake until the cookies are just beginning to brown on the edges, 8 to 10 minutes. Cool on the cookie sheet. Transfer to a wire rack and repeat with the remaining dough.

cream cheese cookies

Sometimes people's first reaction to cream cheese cookies is confusion: "Cream cheese cookies?" they ask. One bite of these rich, smooth cookies and you'll surely be a convert.

2 sticks (½ pound) unsalted butter, at room temperature	1 large egg yolk, at room temperature
4 ounces (1 small package) cream cheese, at room temperature	1 teaspoon vanilla extract
	2½ cups all-purpose flour
1 cup granulated sugar	¾ teaspoon kosher salt

- Preheat the oven to 325°F.
- Place the butter, cream cheese, and sugar in the bowl of a mixer fitted with a paddle and beat until smooth and creamy. Add the egg yolk and vanilla, beating well between additions. Scrape down the sides of the bowl, add the remaining ingredients and beat until everything is well incorporated. Scrape down the sides of the bowl and beat again.
- Drop large teaspoons of dough onto an unbuttered cookie sheet about 2 inches apart and bake until the edges are just beginning to brown, 14 to 16 minutes. Let cool on the sheet. Transfer to a wire rack and repeat with the remaining dough.

COOKIE BAKING TIP ੭≈

Instead of greasing or buttering cookie sheets, we like to line them with parchment paper; it's a great way to ease cleanup and prevent cookies from sticking.

fraya berg's famous biscotti

YIELD: ABOUT **16** DOZEN BISCOTTI

Fraya loves to bake but hates to spend tons of time on it, so this is her go-to recipe. It takes about 10 minutes to make the dough, another 5 to shape the logs and get them in the oven, and then 25 to bake. While one batch is baking, she usually makes another. She slices batch #1 while batch #2 bakes and ends up with piles and piles of biscotti.

During the holidays, Fraya, her friend Jennifer Fish and some of Jennifer's friends spent an entire day mixing, baking, slicing, and bagging 100 pounds of these biscotti. Jennifer gave all of it to her clients as holiday gifts, with a note attached about the mission of Cookies for Kids' Cancer as well as the donation she made to the organization in the client's name. Clients raved about both the biscotti and Jennifer's thoughtfulness.

½ stick (2 ounces) unsalted butter, at room temperature

2 cups granulated sugar

4 large eggs, at room temperature

1 tablespoon anise seed

1 teaspoon vanilla extract

4 cups all-purpose flour

½ teaspoon baking soda

⅛ teaspoon salt

1 pound whole almonds

- Preheat the oven to 350°F. Line 2 cookie sheets with parchment paper.

- Place the butter and sugar in the bowl of a mixer fitted with a paddle and beat until light and fluffy, about 3 minutes. Add the eggs, anise seed and vanilla, one at a time, beating after each addition. With the mixer on low speed, beat in flour, baking soda, and salt until well combined. Add the almonds and mix until just incorporated (it's okay if some of them break).

- Using cold, wet hands, form the dough into 8 balls and then shape each ball into a 10-inch log about 1¼ inches in diameter.

- Place the logs on the prepared cookie sheets about 3 inches apart. Transfer to the oven and bake until just golden, 25 to 30 minutes. Set aside to cool 10 minutes.

- Transfer the cooked logs to a cutting board and using a very sharp straight-edged knife, slice the logs on a slight diagonal, about $1/3$ inch thick. Place the slices on unlined baking sheets and bake until just golden and dry to the touch, 15 to 20 minutes.

- Cool completely. Store in resealable plastic bags or airtight containers at room temperature for 3 to 4 weeks or freeze for up to 3 months.

variation Substitute 4 cups walnuts for the almonds and 1 heaping teaspoon grated fresh orange zest for the anise seed.

BAKE SALE TIP ❧ what do you need for a bake sale?

Baking:
- Recipes
- Shopping lists
- Packaging supplies
- Stickers, tags, or labels

Set up:
- Tables
- Craft paper
- Packing tape
- Banners or signs announcing the bake sale
- Baskets to display baked goods
- Flowers or balloons for the table
- Chairs
- Canopy tent—for shade in the heat or shelter from the rain
- Trays for passing out samples
- Donation jars
- Rubber gloves for handling food

---

prince liam's peanut butter cookies

YIELD: 3 DOZEN COOKIES

Another cookie that people either totally love or totally hate. If you're a peanut butter cookie lover, you will flip for these, developed by pal David Bonom, who gave them their name too. When we asked him why he named them so, he answered "I love these cookies and I love Liam!"

Why shortening? While the purists among you may want to substitute butter for the shortening, be prepared for your peanut butter cookies to have a totally different texture—they'll be soft and sandy rather than crisp and chewy. Also, be sure to combine the flour, baking powder, and salt in a separate bowl before adding to the peanut mixture. This extra step avoids over-mixing the batter, which results in tougher cookies. It is also done to make sure the leavening is distributed evenly in the batter.

½ cup vegetable shortening

½ cup granulated sugar, plus additional for sprinkling

½ cup packed dark brown sugar

½ cup natural-style peanut butter, at room temperature

1 large egg, at room temperature

1 teaspoon vanilla extract

1½ cups unbleached all-purpose flour

1¼ teaspoons baking powder

⅛ teaspoon salt

¾ cup dry roasted peanuts, coarsely chopped

- Preheat the oven to 350°F. Line 3 cookie sheets with parchment paper.

- Place the shortening, sugars, peanut butter, egg, and vanilla in the bowl of a mixer fitted with a paddle and beat on medium speed stopping occasionally to scrape down the sides of the bowl, until well combined, about 3 minutes.

- In a separate bowl, combine the flour, baking powder, and salt. Add the flour mixture to the peanut butter mixture and beat on low speed until well combined, 1 to 2 minutes. Add the peanuts and beat 30 seconds longer.

- Drop the batter by tablespoonfuls on the prepared cookie sheets, about 1½ inches apart. Roll each tablespoon of batter into a ball. Working one at a time, dip the tines of a fork in sugar and press down each ball into a 1½- to 1¾- inch round, forming a crosshatch on top.

- Transfer to the oven and bake until the edges of the cookies are lightly browned, 12 to 14 minutes. Cool cookies on cookie sheet on a rack for 5 minutes. Transfer to the rack and cool completely.

BAKE SALE TIPS *From Donna Reynolds*

- Make your bake sale an annual event—Our town's Christmas celebration includes a festival and parade where we've held bake sales for the past three years. After the first year, people were looking for our tables of goodies and ready to make a donation. By the third year, it was expected we would be there.
- Samples, samples, samples. Don't discard broken cookies. Instead use them as samples for people stopping by. For holiday bake sales, offer complimentary hot cider or hot chocolate to draw in the crowd. A gift of a warm cup of cider on a cold night gets everyone in the giving spirit.
- Because it's almost impossible to say no to kids, we include our local Girl Scout troop in the bake sale. Not only is it a great way for kids to give back, each girl who participates receives the Cookies for Kids' Cancer Girl Scout patch for participating. It's cute and they wear it with pride for their community involvement.

coconut-almond chocolate chip cookies

YIELD: 3 TO 4 DOZEN COOKIES

W atch out, Girl Scouts. These are even more addictive than your famous version!

2 sticks (½ pound) unsalted butter, at room temperature

½ cup granulated sugar

1¼ cup sweetened flaked coconut

1 large egg, at room temperature

2 tablespoons water, at room temperature

1 teaspoon vanilla extract

½ teaspoon almond extract

2 cups all-purpose flour

1 cup quick-cooking or old-fashioned oats

1 teaspoon baking powder

1 teaspoon baking soda

1 teaspoon kosher salt

2 cups semi-sweet chocolate chips

2 cups almonds, toasted (see Tip) and chopped

- Preheat the oven to 325°F. Line a cookie sheet with parchment paper.

- Place the butter, sugar, and coconut in the bowl of a mixer fitted with a paddle and beat until smooth and creamy. Add the egg, water, vanilla, and almond extracts, one at a time, beating well between additions. Scrape down the sides of the bowl. Place the flour, oats, baking powder, baking soda, and salt in a separate bowl, mix well, and add to the butter mixture. Beat until everything is well incorporated. Scrape down the sides of the bowl, then add the chocolate chips and almonds and beat again.

- Form the dough into heaping-teaspoon-size balls and place them about 2 inches apart on the prepared cookie sheet. Using your palm, gently press down. Alternatively, you can roll the dough into a log (see page 4).

- Transfer to the oven and bake until the cookies begin to brown at the edges, 12 to 15 minutes. Cool on the cookie sheet. Transfer to a wire rack and repeat with the remaining dough.

TIP ᘒᕦ To toast nuts, preheat the oven to 350°F. Place the nuts on an ungreased baking pan or cookie sheet and bake until golden, 10 to 15 minutes (depending on the nut).

BAKE SALE TIP ᘒᕦ

Bake Sale Philosophy—Get it donated!
Sugar, flour, butter, eggs.
Chocolate, nuts, butterscotch, coconut.
Bags, ribbon, paper, balloons.
What do these all have in common? All of them are items that can be donated to a bake sale.

Be inspired to host an amazing bake sale, but don't let your bake sale break the bank. Start your bake sale planning by writing a simple request for donations. Take that letter to everyone you know—your grocery store, housewares store, local bakeries, and even specialty gift shops. Be sure to tell them you are hosting a bake sale for a nonprofit organization. You will be amazed how often stores say yes. Grocery stores might offer gift cards to cover the cost of supplies or will simply fulfill your shopping list. Housewares stores might support with a donation of extra baskets for the display or decorative items for the table. Gift shops might donate fun prizes for a raffle. Essentially, the more you engage your community by seeking support, the more you spread the word about the cause and get everyone involved.

adina's classic black-and-white cookies

YIELD: ABOUT 6 DOZEN COOKIES

A dina's cookies, which always sell out quickly, require cake flour, which you may not have on hand. It's worth buying cake flour just for these cookies because we guarantee they'll become a regular, whether at bake sales, birthday celebrations, picnics, or dinner parties.

for the cookies

2 sticks (½ pound) unsalted butter, at room temperature

1¾ cups granulated sugar

4 large eggs, at room temperature

1 cup whole milk (please don't substitute low-fat milk)

1 teaspoon vanilla extract

2½ cups cake flour

2½ cups all-purpose flour

1 teaspoon baking powder

for the icing

4 cups confectioners' sugar

⅓ cup boiling water

1 ounce bittersweet chocolate, melted

- Preheat the oven to 375°F. Line 2 cookie sheets with parchment paper.

- Place the butter and sugar in a mixer fitted with a paddle and beat until light and fluffy. Add the eggs, one at a time, mixing well between additions. Add the milk and vanilla and beat well. Place the flours and baking powder in a bowl and mix well. With the mixer running, gradually add the dry ingredients to the butter mixture and beat until completely mixed.

- Form the dough into tablespoon-size balls and place about 2 inches apart on the prepared cookie sheets. Transfer to the oven and bake until the edges of the cookies just begin to brown, about 15 minutes. Transfer to a wire rack and repeat with the remaining dough.

- **To make the icing:** Place the confectioners' sugar in a large mixing bowl and add the water, 1 tablespoon at a time, until the mixture is spreadable but still thick. Transfer half the icing to another mixing bowl and stir in the melted chocolate. Set aside to cool.

- Spread half the rounded side (flat sides down) of the cookies with white icing and the other half with the chocolate icing. Set aside until the icing hardens completely.

BAKE SALE TIP ॐ offer cookie decorating

What's the most important ingredient at a Cookies for Kids' Cancer bake sale? Why, kids, of course!

We love kids at bake sales. Not only are children the inspiration, they bring fun, silliness, and love to the bake sale table. Our favorite way to attract the littlest of supporters is to offer a Cookie Decorating Table.

All you need:
- One extra table, covered with craft paper
- Baked sugar cookies, plus napkins or paper towels
- Waxed paper cut into squares (great for anything with icing)
- Multiple containers of icing, sprinkles, colored sugars, and candies for decorating
- Donation jar
- Lots of wet wipes

While some children will decorate and eat their cookies in a flash, others will use cookie decorating as an opportunity to express themselves artistically. As the kids decorate their cookies, use the time to talk to their parents—share why you are hosting a bake sale, what inspired you to get involved, and how the supporter's donation will make a difference.

Make local connections. If you're holding a bake sale to support a specific child in the area, tell that child's story. Make the connection between the child and the effort.

---

double-chocolate biscotti with almonds

YIELD: 7 TO 8 DOZEN BISCOTTI

C ocoa powder plus chocolate chips helps make a wonderfully rich, yet still light biscotti.

6 large eggs

2 cups granulated sugar

2 teaspoons vanilla extract

4 cups all-purpose flour

¾ cup unsweetened cocoa powder

2 teaspoons baking soda

1 teaspoon kosher salt

2 cups semi-sweet chocolate chips

2 cups almonds or hazelnuts, lightly toasted (see Tip page 17) and coarsely chopped

- Preheat the oven to 350°F. Line 2 baking sheets with parchment paper.

- Place the eggs, sugar, and vanilla in the bowl of a mixer fitted with a paddle and beat until light and fluffy, about 3 minutes. Place the flour, cocoa powder, baking soda, and salt in a separate bowl, mix well, and add to the egg mixture. Gently pulse until well combined. Scrape down the sides of the bowl, add the chocolate chips and almonds, and beat well.

- Using cold, wet hands, form the dough into 4 balls and then shape each ball into a 10-inch log about 1¼ inches in diameter.

- Place the logs on the prepared baking sheets about 3 inches apart. Transfer to the oven and bake until the tops begin to crack, 25 to 30 minutes. Set aside to cool for 10 minutes.

- Transfer the cooked logs to a cutting board and using a very sharp straight-edged knife, slice the logs on a slight diagonal, about $1/3$ inch thick. Place the slices on unlined baking sheets and bake until just dry to the touch, 15 to 20 minutes.

- Cool completely. Store in airtight containers at room temperature for 3 to 4 weeks or freeze for up to 3 months.

variation Add ½ cup coarsely chopped coffee beans.

tried-and-true sparkly ginger snaps

YIELD: 3 TO 4 DOZEN COOKIES ᘒ

If you are hosting or contributing to a cookie exchange, don't forget these impossible-to-eat-just-one favorites. Be sure to package them by the half-dozen or dozen to give your bake sale supporter enough cookies to enjoy on the way home with some left to share later. If you are having a summer bake sale, consider making homemade ice cream for your bake sale and pair it with Sparkly Ginger Snap crumbles for the perfect topping.

for the sparkly ginger sugar

3 tablespoons granulated sugar

¾ teaspoon ground ginger

for the cookies

1 stick (¼ pound) unsalted butter, at room temperature

¾ cup plus 2 tablespoons granulated sugar

1 large egg, at room temperature

3 tablespoons dark molasses

2 cups all-purpose flour

1 tablespoon ground ginger

1½ teaspoons baking soda

½ teaspoon ground cinnamon

¼ teaspoon kosher salt

- Preheat the oven to 350°F. Line a cookie sheet with parchment paper.

- **To make the sparkly ginger sugar:** Place the sugar and ginger on a plate and mix until combined. Set aside.

- **To make the cookies:** Place the butter and sugar in the bowl of a mixer fitted with a paddle and beat until smooth and creamy. Add the egg and molasses, one at a time, beating well between additions. Scrape down the sides of the bowl. Place the flour, ginger, baking soda, cinnamon, and salt in a separate bowl and mix well. Add to the butter mixture and beat until everything is well incorporated. Scrape down the sides of the bowl and beat again.

- Break off small pieces and roll into 1-inch balls. Roll the balls in the sparkly ginger sugar and place 2 inches apart on the prepared cookie sheet. Using your hand or the bottom of a water glass, press down until flattened. Transfer to the oven and bake until the cookies begin to brown at the edges, 12 to 15 minutes. Cool on the cookie sheet. Transfer the cookies to a wire rack and repeat with the remaining dough.

BAKE SALE TIP host a holiday cookie exchange

Molasses cookies are a favorite at Holiday Cookie Exchanges: parties where everyone attending brings cookies to share and goes home with a variety of cookies for holiday entertaining. If you're looking for a way to raise funds with friends, consider hosting a Cookie Exchange.

Ask your friends to make one type of cookie (3 to 4 dozen) to bring to the exchange. As guests arrive, set all the cookies out on a large table. After mingling, chatting about the cause, and snacking on savory treats, distribute take-home bags adorned with holiday colors and a Cookies for Kids' Cancer sticker. Guests make their way around the table, going clockwise. First time around, pick up one cookie from any tray; next time, pick up two cookies from any tray. Continue going around the table until all the cookies have been claimed. Then, all the guests make a donation to Cookies for Kids' Cancer and go home with a bag filled with treats to share during the holidays.

---

crunchy, spicy, decidedly grown-up molasses cookies

YIELD: 3 TO 4 DOZEN COOKIES ᘒ

Although these are terrific sellers all year round, they scream HOLIDAYS so don't even think of omitting them at any winter bake sales.

1½ sticks (6 ounces) unsalted butter, at room temperature

1 cup granulated sugar, plus additional for rolling

1 large egg, at room temperature

¼ cup blackstrap molasses

1 teaspoon vanilla extract

2 cups all-purpose flour

2 teaspoons baking soda

½ teaspoon kosher salt

½ teaspoon ground cinnamon

½ teaspoon ground ginger

¼ teaspoon ground cardamom

- Preheat the oven to 375°F. Line a cookie sheet with parchment paper.

- Place the butter and sugar in the bowl of a mixer fitted with a paddle and beat until smooth and creamy. Add the egg, molasses, and vanilla, one at a time, beating well between additions. Scrape down the sides of the bowl. Place the flour, baking soda, salt, and spices in a separate bowl and mix well. Add to the butter mixture. Beat until everything is well incorporated. Scrape down the sides of the bowl and beat again.

- To form the cookies, break off small pieces and roll into 1-inch balls. Roll the balls in the sugar and place 2 inches apart on the prepared cookie sheet. Using your hand or the bottom of a water glass, press down until flattened. Alternatively, you can roll the dough into a log (see Tip, page 4). Transfer to the oven and bake until the cookies begin to brown at the edges, 12 to 15 minutes. Cool on the cookie sheet. Transfer to a wire rack and repeat with the remaining dough.

pecan sandies

Old-fashioned and yummy, these nutty, buttery cookies are extremely popular at bake sales and cookie exchanges. Plus they are sturdy and hold up well when transported.

3 sticks (¾ pound) unsalted butter, at room temperature

1 cup granulated sugar

2 large eggs, at room temperature

1 tablespoon vanilla extract

1 tablespoon water, at room temperature

4 cups all-purpose flour

1½ teaspoons kosher salt

¼ teaspoon baking soda

2½ cups pecans, lightly toasted (see Tip page 17) and coarsely chopped

- Preheat the oven to 325°F.

- Place the butter and sugar in the bowl of a mixer fitted with a paddle and beat until smooth and creamy. Add the eggs, vanilla, and water, one at a time, beating well between additions. Scrape down the sides of the bowl. Place the flour, salt, and baking soda in a separate bowl and mix well. Add to the butter mixture and beat until combined. Scrape down the sides of the bowl, add the pecans, and beat again.

- Form the dough into 1-inch balls and, using your hand or the bottom of a water glass, press down until flattened. Place on an ungreased cookie sheet. Transfer to the oven and bake until the cookies are just beginning to brown on the edges, 17 to 20 minutes. Transfer to a wire cooling rack. Let the cookie sheet cool completely between batches and repeat with the remaining dough.

Julie Sussman, Washington, D.C.

In the 2½ years I've been holding Cookies for Kids' Cancer bake sales, the most memorable moment was the day before Mother's Day when my friend and her husband arrived with arms full of homemade baked goods. This couple has two sons, one of whom has been fighting cancer since fifth grade and is now a sophomore in high school. The mom did all the talking and the dad stayed silent. I sensed something was amiss, but I figured if something were wrong, then they certainly wouldn't have baked! It wasn't until later that day that I learned that their son's cancer had returned for a fourth time. I was devastated to learn the news and humbled by the strength and commitment of my friends to end pediatric cancer. They put their own pain and heartache to the side, baked, wrapped, and then steeled themselves to donate the goods, as well as thank all of us for what we were doing, without once letting on about their personal tragedy.

They are my heroes. And that's why I hold bake sales.

Debi Donoho, Mansfield, TX

Our Cookies for Kids' Cancer bake sales we have had have always been a group effort for me and my sisters, even though we live in different cities. We all love to cook and bake, are passionate about children, and understand how desperately they need better cancer treatments. We were struggling to find a way to make our first bake sale effective. We couldn't really find a date or time that worked for all three of us, neither of us had a large kitchen to do major baking, and we didn't know of an adequate venue to host a bake sale. After some brainstorming, our solution was a "No-Bake Sale." "No-Bake Cookies" were our favorite cookies as kids, and my grandmother made wonderful no-bakes—we often made them with her. Each of us had made these for friends in the past, and everyone always loved them. We sent an email to everyone we knew explaining Cookies for Kids' Cancer and asking our friends, family, and co-workers to buy at least one dozen cookies from us. We offered to personally deliver or send them. Within a day, we had orders for more than 25 dozen. The orders continued to come in over the coming weeks, exceeding our goals.

Brandi and Scott Phillips, Tulsa, OK

Our inspiration for getting involved with Cookies for Kids' Cancer is our amazing son, Pierce Alexander Phillips, aka "Super Pierce." Pierce was diagnosed with stage 3 high-risk neuroblastoma on August 26, 2008, at 13 months old. After a 14 month battle, Pierce earned his angel wings on October 9, 2009, at the young age of 27 months old.

We want all kids to have a chance to have as many birthdays as possible. So we decided to help raise funds for kids who so badly deserve more options. One thing that helped make our bake sales a success was to have it in a nice shopping center in front of multiple stores. We advertised on the radio and at the stores and were so happy with the response from the community. Everyone wanted to help. After all, it is up to us to find a cure!

dried cranberry and chocolate cookies

YIELD: **3** TO **4** DOZEN COOKIES

Tart and rich, these crunchy cookies are reminiscent of chocolate chip cookies.

2½ sticks (10 ounces) unsalted butter, at room temperature

1 cup light brown sugar

½ cup granulated sugar

1 large egg, at room temperature

1 large egg yolk, at room temperature

1 tablespoon vanilla extract

2 cups all-purpose flour

1 cup quick-cooking or old-fashioned rolled oats

1 teaspoon baking powder

1 teaspoon baking soda

1 teaspoon kosher salt

1½ cups chocolate chips, either semi-sweet or white chocolate

1½ cups dried cranberries

- Preheat the oven to 325°F. Line a cookie sheet with parchment paper.

- Place the butter and sugars in the bowl of a mixer fitted with a paddle and beat until smooth and creamy. Add the egg, egg yolk, and vanilla, one at a time, beating well between additions. Scrape down the sides of the bowl. Place the flour, oats, baking powder, baking soda, and salt in a separate bowl and mix well. Add to the butter mixture and beat until everything is well incorporated. Scrape down the sides of the bowl, add the chocolate chips and cranberries and beat again.

- Drop the dough by heaping teaspoons about 2 inches apart on the prepared cookie sheet. Transfer to the oven and bake until the cookies begin to brown at the edges, 12 to 15 minutes. Cool on the cookie sheet. Transfer to a wire rack and repeat with the remaining dough.

brown sugar cookies

Another great variation on the classic sugar cookie, this version is just a little deeper and richer than its inspiration.

1½ sticks (6 ounces) unsalted butter, at room temperature

1¼ cups dark brown sugar

1 large egg, at room temperature

2 cups all-purpose flour

2 teaspoons baking soda

½ teaspoon kosher salt

½ teaspoon ground ginger

½ teaspoon ground cinnamon

- Preheat the oven to 375°F.

- Place the butter and sugar in the bowl of a mixer fitted with a paddle and beat until smooth and creamy. Add the egg and beat well. Scrape down the sides of the bowl. Place the flour, baking soda, salt, and spices in a separate bowl and mix well. Add to the butter mixture and beat until everything is well incorporated. Scrape down the sides of the bowl and beat again.

- Drop large teaspoonfuls of dough onto an unbuttered cookie sheet about 2 inches apart and bake until the edges are just brown, 8 to 12 minutes. For crispy cookies, let cool on the sheet. Let the cookie sheet cool completely between batches and repeat with the remaining dough.

BROWN SUG
COOKIES

cinnamon-sugared snickerdoodles

YIELD: **3** TO **4** DOZEN COOKIES ૨➛

S nickerdoodles are another bake-sale must. Patrons love the cinnamon topping with the added sugary crunch.

for the cinnamon sugar

2 tablespoons granulated sugar

1 tablespoon ground cinnamon

for the cookies

2 sticks (½ pound) unsalted butter, margarine, shortening or a blend, at room temperature

1½ cups granulated sugar

2 large eggs, at room temperature

2¾ cups all-purpose flour

2 teaspoons cream of tartar

1 teaspoon baking soda

½ teaspoon kosher salt

- **To make the cinnamon sugar:** Place the sugar and cinnamon on a plate and mix until combined. Set aside.

- **To make the cookies:** Place the butter and sugar in the bowl of a mixer fitted with a paddle and beat until smooth and creamy. Add the eggs, one at a time, beating well between additions. Scrape down the sides of the bowl. Place the flour, cream of tartar, baking soda, and salt in a separate bowl and mix well. Add to the butter mixture and beat until everything is well incorporated. Scrape down the sides of the bowl and beat again. Cover and refrigerate at least 2 hours and up to overnight.

- Preheat the oven to 350°F. Line a cookie sheet with parchment paper.

- **To form the cookies:** Break off small pieces of dough and roll into 1-inch balls. Roll the balls in the cinnamon sugar and place 2 inches apart on the prepared cookie sheet. Using your hand or the bottom of a water glass, press down until flattened.

- Transfer to the oven and bake until the cookies begin to brown at the edges, 8 to 10 minutes. Cool on the cookie sheet. Transfer to a wire rack and repeat with the remaining dough.

lemon zest shortbread cookies

YIELD: ABOUT **6** DOZEN COOKIES ⮑

L emon lovers will jump on this one! Actually you don't even have to be a lemon lover: Liam Witt, the inspiration behind Cookies for Kids' Cancer, fell in love with these cookies as soon as he laid eyes on them. No one ever doubted which cookie Liam was craving when he asked for "yellow cookies."

4 sticks (1 pound) unsalted butter, at room temperature

⅔ cup confectioners' sugar

⅔ cup granulated sugar

Grated zest of 6 well-washed lemons

2 teaspoons vanilla extract

4½ cups all-purpose flour

2 teaspoons kosher salt

- Place the butter, sugars, grated zest, and vanilla in the bowl of a mixer fitted with a paddle and beat until smooth and creamy. Scrape down the sides of the bowl, slowly (or the flour will poof up all around you) add the remaining ingredients and beat until everything is well incorporated. Scrape down the sides of the bowl and beat again.

- Form into two 1½-inch-diameter logs and cover with parchment paper. Place the logs in a resealable plastic bag and refrigerate at least 1 hour and up to 2 days, or freeze up to 2 months.

- Preheat the oven to 325°F. Line a cookie sheet with parchment paper.

- With the tip of a very sharp knife, cut ⅜-inch slices of the dough and place 2 inches apart on the prepared cookie sheet. Transfer to the oven and bake until the cookies are just beginning to brown on the edges, about 20 minutes. Transfer to a wire rack to cool. Let the cookie sheet cool completely between batches and repeat with the remaining dough.

mexican wedding cookies

Mexican Wedding Cookies are known by many names—Italian Wedding Cookies, Greek Wedding Cookies, Viennese Cookies, and, with a slight change of shape, they are known as Crescents. No matter the region, origin, or slight differences in recipes, all these cookies share common traits and are traditionally served at special occasions such as the holidays or a wedding.

2 sticks (½ pound) unsalted butter, at room temperature

¼ cup confectioners' sugar, plus additional for rolling

1 teaspoon vanilla extract

2 cups all-purpose flour

2 cups walnut halves, lightly toasted (see Tip page 17), cooled, and finely ground

- Preheat the oven to 375°F.

- Place the butter, sugar, and vanilla in the bowl of a mixer fitted with a paddle and beat until smooth and creamy. Scrape down the sides of the bowl, slowly add the remaining ingredients, and beat until everything is well incorporated. Scrape down the sides of the bowl and beat again.

- Form the dough into 1-inch balls and place 2 inches apart on an unbuttered cookie sheet. Transfer to the oven and bake until the cookies are just beginning to lightly brown on the edges, about 15 minutes. Transfer the cookies to a wire rack, cool, and then roll in confectioners' sugar. Repeat with the remaining dough, letting the cookie sheet cool completely between batches.

2014

almost black they're so cocoa cookies

YIELD: ABOUT 5 DOZEN COOKIES

There's always one great chocolate cookie at a bake sale and this one is a must.

Use the very best unsweetened cocoa powder you can find: don't even think of substituting the sweetened variety: save that for mixing into hot milk! At Christmas, try substituting the nuts with broken peppermint sticks. The combination is glorious. *delicious!!!*

2 sticks (½ pound) unsalted butter, at room temperature

1 cup granulated sugar

2 large eggs, at room temperature

1 tablespoon vanilla extract

2 cups all-purpose flour

1 cup unsweetened cocoa powder

1 teaspoon baking soda

½ teaspoon baking powder

½ teaspoon kosher salt

1½ cups walnuts, pecans, or hazelnuts, lightly toasted (see Tip page 17) and coarsely chopped *optional*

- Preheat the oven to 350°F. Line a cookie sheet with a Silpat or parchment paper.

- Place the butter and sugar in the bowl of a mixer fitted with a paddle and beat until smooth and creamy. Add the eggs, and vanilla, one at a time, beating well between additions. Scrape down the sides of the bowl. Place the flour, cocoa powder, baking soda, baking powder, and salt in a separate bowl and mix well. Gradually add to the butter mixture and beat until everything is well incorporated. Scrape down the sides of the bowl and beat again. *Add nuts.*

- Place heaping teaspoonfuls of dough 2 inches apart on the prepared cookie sheet and transfer to the oven. Bake until the edges begin to firm up, 12 to 14 minutes; do not overbake. For crispy cookies, let cool on the cookie sheet. Transfer to a wire rack and repeat with the remaining dough.

Jennifer Fish, Oakland, CA

As soon as I heard about Cookies for Kids' Cancer, I knew I wanted to get involved. My first bake sale couldn't have been easier: I baked cookies and put a donation jar out at the office. In an hour, all the cookies were gone and I'd collected $143, which my company matched. Since that first bake sale, I've gone on to coordinate many more, each a huge and rewarding success. I marvel at how everyone who helps

me then thanks *me* for letting them help. It just makes you feel good to get involved.

Erica O'Connor, Erie, CO

At 2½ years old, my daughter Sydney was diagnosed with ovarian cancer, a frightening diagnosis, and we are blessed to report Sydney is now a thriving six-year old.

Since this life changing experience, I wanted to do something to make a difference and get involved with pediatric cancer. I loved the story of how Cookies for Kids' Cancer started. I love the concept. I feel it is doable for me. And I believe we all, whether big or small, can make a difference. My bake sale was a fun, uplifting, inspiring experience.

Having my cancer-survivor daughter help me during the bake sale was important and special. My youngest daughter, Avery, who is 3, was such a trooper on both days at the sale. I can still hear her sweet voice walking up to people and asking, "Do you want a sticker for Cookies for Kids' Cancer?"

There were many times I got choked up because of the kindness and generosity of people. Some would walk up and just want to donate without taking any baked goods. There was about an hour during my bake sale that many of my friends showed up individually during that time, and I remember one of my girlfriends making a generous donation and telling me,

"Thank you for doing this. You are such an incredible woman." I started to cry.

I raised around $3,300! My goal was to raise $2,000.

Chelsey Fields, New York, NY

We had a magical location in a park and our bakers made delicious and outstanding treats to sell. We set up "Decorate Your Own Cookie" and "Mother's Day Card" tables to raise even more! We had mothers and fathers and babies coming to bake, sell, or help in any way they had the time. There were samples being shared and people were so generous to us and the cause. We planned to have a variety of treats for our more sensitive customers,

Mississippi State University chapters of Alpha Epsilon Delta and Beta Beta Beta, Starkville, MS

The Mississippi State University chapters of Alpha Epsilon Delta (Health Pre-professional Honor Society) and Tri-Beta (National Biology Honor Society) joined forces to co-sponsor a campus-wide bake sale/fundraiser. The majority of our members are either biology majors or health-related pre-professionals. We are often looking for a "big" spring project to participate in. We were excited with the concept of a fundraiser that would help to promote the ideals of our clubs. In less than four weeks of planning and a day-long bake sale, we executed a very successful event. Contributions were made by students, faculty, and staff, as well as local businesses. We were astonished by and very appreciative of the generosity and positive responses we received from others.

including gluten-free, sugar-free, and some vegan. These were the most requested items and we will definitely plan for the next sale. It was truly a busy day in the park, and I recall at one point just stopping and reflecting on all the other people in the park right around us. There were musicians set up and playing music, there was a group of drama students who chose our spot in the park to perform their interpretations of various art. I knew this would be translated into lots of money raised for cookies and the cause. We raised close to $10,000 that day, and then through corporate matching progams, doubled the amount to nearly $20,000. It was an incredible amount of effort that was incredibly rewarding!

fresh apple
cranberry bars

classic chewy brownies

YIELD: **2** DOZEN BROWNIES

Brownies and bars can be cut into shapes using your favorite cookie cutters. It will add interest to the packaging of the baked good.

Brownies and bars also ship very well because they are denser than most cookies. So if your supporters want to use them as a gift to someone far away, assist them in creating a variety pack and encourage them to take a brochure to enclose in their goodie box. It is a great way to make someone's day as well as spread the word about Cookies for Kids' Cancer.

2 sticks (½ pound) unsalted butter	2 teaspoons vanilla extract
¼ pound unsweetened chocolate, coarsely chopped	¾ cup all-purpose flour
	¼ teaspoon kosher salt
1¾ cups granulated sugar	1½ cups walnuts or pecans (optional), coarsely chopped
4 large eggs, at room temperature	

- Preheat the oven to 325°F. Lightly butter a 9 x 13-inch pan and line it with parchment paper, allowing enough overhang on the long side to lift the brownies from the pan.

- Place the butter and chocolate in a small saucepan and cook, stirring, over the lowest possible heat until both are melted, 3 to 5 minutes. Set aside to cool.

- Place the sugar, eggs, and vanilla in a large mixing bowl and stir until just combined. Add the cooled chocolate mixture and stir until just combined. Add the flour and salt and stir until just combined. Pour into the prepared pan and sprinkle with the nuts, if desired.

- Transfer to the oven and bake until your kitchen smells like chocolate and a toothpick inserted in the center comes out clean, 25 to 30 minutes. Set aside to cool and cut into 24 bars.

chocolate chip walnut brownies

YIELD: 2 DOZEN BROWNIES

A classic brownie made more decadent by the addition of chocolate chips and walnuts.

To hasten the cooling of the chocolate, place the saucepan in a larger pan or bowl of cold water and stir occasionally.

2 sticks (½ pound) unsalted butter

½ pound semi-sweet chocolate, coarsely chopped

3 ounces unsweetened chocolate, coarsely chopped

1 cup plus 2 tablespoons granulated sugar

3 large eggs, at room temperature

1 tablespoon vanilla extract

¾ cup all-purpose flour

1½ teaspoons baking powder

½ teaspoon kosher salt

1 to 1½ cups walnuts or pecans, coarsely chopped

1 cup semi-sweet chocolate chips

- Preheat the oven to 350°F. Lightly butter a 9 x 13-inch pan and line with parchment paper, allowing enough overhang on the long side to lift the brownies from the pan.

- Place the butter and chocolates in a small saucepan and cook, stirring, over the lowest possible heat until melted, 3 to 5 minutes. Set aside to cool.

- Place the sugar, eggs, and vanilla in a large mixing bowl and stir until just combined. Add the cooled chocolate mixture and stir until just combined. Place the flour, baking powder, and salt in a separate bowl, mix well, and add to the sugar mixture. Stir until the color of the batter is consistent, with no white streaks. Pour into the prepared pan and sprinkle with the nuts and chocolate chips.

- Transfer to the oven and bake until your kitchen smells like chocolate and a toothpick inserted in the center comes out clean, 30 to 35 minutes. Set aside to cool to room temperature, then cover and refrigerate. When the brownies are fully cooled, cut into 24 squares.

intense dense dark cocoa brownies

YIELD: 2 DOZEN BROWNIES

Instead of the more commonly used chocolate, these brownies use lots and lots of unsweetened cocoa powder, helping to create the most intense, dense brownies.

2 sticks (½ pound) unsalted butter, at room temperature

1 cup granulated sugar

1 cup light brown sugar

3 large eggs, at room temperature

1 tablespoon vanilla extract

1⅔ cups unsweetened cocoa powder

1⅓ cups all-purpose flour

½ teaspoon kosher salt

2 cups pecans, lightly toasted (see Tip page 17) and coarsely chopped

- Preheat the oven to 325°F. Lightly butter a 9 x 13-inch pan and line with parchment paper, allowing enough overhang on the long side to lift the brownies from the pan.

- Place the butter and sugars in the bowl of a mixer fitted with a paddle and beat until creamy. Add the eggs, and vanilla, one at a time, beating well after each addition. Place the cocoa powder, flour, and salt in a separate bowl, mix, and add to the butter mixture. Pulse on the lowest speed to combine (if you don't do this gradually, the dry ingredients will fly all over the place). Scrape down the sides and beat again.

- Transfer to the prepared pan and spread evenly with a spatula. (It will seem like it's too thick and will be hard to spread, but this is how it should be.)

- Transfer to the oven and bake until a toothpick inserted in the center comes out dry, about 25 minutes. Set aside to cool COMPLETELY and cut into 24 bars.

dark rich mocha-glazed brownies

YIELD: **2 DOZEN BROWNIES**

E ven with the fabulous mocha glaze, these dark rich brownies are not overly sweet. Don't be tempted to leave it off; it's a large part of what makes these so spectacular.

Make these brownies when you don't have a ton of time: luckily they get better as they age, up to 3 days.

for the brownies

10 tablespoons (5 ounces) unsalted butter

12 ounces bitter or semi-sweet chocolate

4 large eggs, at room temperature

1½ cups granulated sugar

1 tablespoon vanilla extract

1⅓ cups all-purpose flour

¼ cup unsweetened cocoa powder

1 teaspoon baking powder

½ teaspoon kosher salt

for the glaze

1 tablespoon unsalted butter

2 teaspoons light corn syrup

⅔ cup confectioners' sugar

⅓ cup water or prepared coffee

6 ounces semi-sweet chocolate

2 ounces unsweetened chocolate

2 teaspoons vanilla extract

- Preheat the oven to 350°F. Lightly butter a 9 x 13-inch pan and line with parchment paper, allowing enough overhang on the long side to lift the brownies from the pan.

- **To make the brownies:** Place the butter and chocolate in a small saucepan over the lowest possible heat and cook until almost all the chocolate has melted. Off heat, stir until smooth. Set aside to cool to room temperature.

- Place the eggs, sugar, and vanilla in the bowl of a mixer fitted with a whisk attachment and whip until lemon-colored and thick. Replace the whisk attachment with the paddle. Place the flour, cocoa powder, baking powder, and salt in a separate bowl, mix well, and add to the egg mixture. Pulse on the lowest speed to combine (if you don't do this gradually, the dry ingredients will fly all over the place). Scrape down the sides of the bowl, add the cooled chocolate mixture, and beat until just combined.

- Pour into the prepared pan, smooth with a knife, and transfer to the oven. Bake until the top is crackly and a tester inserted in the center comes out with a bit of crumb, 20 to 25 minutes. Be careful not to overbake. Cool in the pan for about 20 minutes and then carefully remove as a whole. Set aside to continue cooling.

- **To make the glaze:** Combine the butter, corn syrup, sugar, and water in a small saucepan and bring to a boil over medium heat. Lower the heat to very low, add the chocolates and vanilla and stir until smooth and glossy. Set aside to cool to room temperature.

- After the brownies have cooled, spread evenly with the glaze. Cut into 24 bars.

BAKE SALE TIP ぞ table signage

Use either place cards or small tent cards to write the names of each baked goodie. Indicate those with nuts or if your bake sale is nut-free. If a recipe is a secret family recipe, make a sign to let people know! Remind people with signs that 100% of all bake sale donations goes directly to Cookies for Kids' Cancer, a charity that funds pediatric cancer research.

Nicole Flowers, Boerne, TX

Sometimes we feel helpless when faced with things we have no control over or cannot change. We want to do something; something to help, to make a difference. My stepdaughter's little girl, Dorothy, was diagnosed with cancer at the age of 1½. It was a devastating blow to our family. We all felt very helpless. When we heard about Cookies for Kids' Cancer, we set out to raise money and awareness for pediatric cancer research with a bake sale. We solicited help from everyone we knew, we secured a fantastic location at our town's big street fair, and we did everything we could to spread the word. Signs were posted everywhere, even in local shops and businesses. Press releases were sent to all the local papers, and we sent letters asking for donations from local businesses. The support was overwhelming. We did not set prices for our baked goods. We let people search their

hearts and give whatever amount they wanted. The results were amazing. We raised over $5,000 in one day. During our bake sale, we met adult survivors of pediatric cancer, people with family members currently fighting this disease, and survivors of all types of cancer who were so glad to give. There was not one moment that wasn't meaningful, special, or didn't make us teary-eyed. Absolutely everything was awe-inspiring.

Amber Van Der Meer, Midlothian, VA

I was inspired to host a Cookies for Kids' Cancer bake sale by my amazing son, Ber (age 6), who is battling childhood cancer. The event was at a fitness and wellness center where I work. The club was very willing to let us set up in front on a busy Saturday morning and to post signage before the event. I sent copies of the flyer to the local schools and emailed it to everyone, asking them to share it. Yes, selling

how appreciative the volunteers were. Here I was asking them to help me and they were thanking me for giving them a way to help at a time when they felt helpless. I guess it was a win-win!

Jordyn Weinberg,
Royal Oak, MI

I became involved in Cookies for Kids' Cancer because I love helping people and cooking/baking. I held three bake sales. It was extremely successful and rewarding. The most rewarding part of this experience is knowing that I helped other kids. Of course with every bake sale, there has to be a little taste-testing too!

cookies at a gym may seem a little strange, but it worked! My friend told people how many cookies to bake (about 4 dozen), what type, and asked that they bag and label them (4 or 5 depending on size). People were very generous with their donations. Kids came with the change from their piggy banks. The thing that impacted me the most about hosting the sale was

blondies

Looks like a brownie, cooks like a brownie, but has no chocolate. Okay, this one has white chocolate but we don't count that since white chocolate has no cocoa in it.

1 stick (¼ pound) unsalted butter	1½ teaspoons vanilla extract
2 cups white chocolate chips, divided	2 cups all-purpose flour
1 cup dark brown sugar	1 teaspoon kosher salt
2 large eggs, at room temperature	1 cup walnuts, toasted (see Tip page 17) and lightly chopped

- Preheat the oven to 350°F. Lightly butter a 9 x 13-inch pan and line with parchment paper, allowing enough overhang on the long side to lift the blondies from the pan.

- Place the butter and 1 cup chocolate chips in a small saucepan over the lowest possible heat and cook until almost all the chocolate has melted. Off heat, stir until smooth. Set aside to cool to room temperature.

- Place the sugar, eggs, and vanilla in the bowl of a mixer fitted with a whisk attachment and whip until lemon-colored and thick. Replace the whisk attachment with the paddle and add the flour, salt, walnuts, and remaining 1 cup chocolate chips and beat on the lowest speed until just combined. Scrape down the sides of the bowl, add the cooled chocolate mixture, and beat until just combined.

- Pour into the prepared pan, smooth with a knife, and transfer to the oven. Bake until the top is just beginning to brown and a tester inserted in the center comes out clean, 20 to 22 minutes. Be careful not to overbake. Cool in the pan slightly and then cut into 24 bars.

espresso brownies

Move over, mocha. These brownies get their intense coffee flavor from espresso; feel free to play with the amount to make them as coffee-d as you like.

1½ sticks (6 ounces) unsalted butter	1 cup all-purpose flour
4 ounces bitter or semi-sweet chocolate, chopped	½ cup walnuts, toasted (see Tip page 17) and lightly ground
1 to 2 tablespoons coarsely ground espresso beans	¼ teaspoon kosher salt
3 large eggs, at room temperature	1 cup walnuts, coarsely chopped
1½ cups granulated sugar	

- Preheat the oven to 350°F. Lightly butter a 9 x 13-inch pan and line with parchment paper, allowing enough overhang on the long side to lift the brownies from the pan.

- Place the butter and chocolate in a small saucepan over the lowest possible heat and cook until almost all the chocolate has melted. Off heat, add the ground coffee beans and stir until smooth. Set aside to cool to room temperature.

- Place the eggs and sugar in the bowl of a mixer fitted with a whisk attachment and beat until lemon-colored and thick. Replace the whisk attachment with the paddle and add the flour, ground walnuts, and salt and beat on the lowest speed until just incorporated. Scrape down the sides of the bowl, add the cooled chocolate mixture, and beat until just combined.

- Pour into the prepared pan, smooth with a knife, and sprinkle with the chopped walnuts. Transfer to the oven and bake until the top is just beginning to brown and a tester inserted into the center comes out clean, about 20 to 22 minutes. Be careful not to overbake. Set aside to cool and then cut into 24 pieces.

classic—you can't have a bake sale without—crispy rice treats

YIELD: 24 TREATS ⅋

The name says it all.

2 tablespoons unsalted butter

4 cups mini marshmallows

6 cups crispy rice cereal

2 cups chocolate chips, health bars, M&Ms, or peanut butter chips (optional)

- Lightly butter a 9 x 13-inch pan and line with parchment paper, allowing enough overhang on the long side to lift the treats out of the pan. Lightly butter a metal spatula.

- Place the butter in a skillet over very low heat, and when it has melted, add 3 cups marshmallows and cook until melted, stirring from time to time. Add the remaining 1 cup marshmallows, crispy rice cereal, and the chips, if desired, and quickly mix with a spatula. Transfer to the prepared pan and pat down with your hands into an even layer. Set aside to cool and cut into 24 bars.

BAKE SALE TIP ⅋ **think mini**

Mini muffins, mini cupcakes, small cookies, mini Bundt cakes. Portions that can be eaten on the go in one or two bites or by small mouths are ideal for bake sales. Often people will be walking by when they see a bake sale and want to indulge in a sweet treat immediately.

five-layer bars

This old-fashioned classic has many renditions but we love this one best; feel free to substitute milk, white, butterscotch, or bittersweet chocolate chips for the semi-sweet and almonds, walnuts, or peanuts for the pecans.

1 stick (¼ pound) unsalted butter, melted

2 sleeves graham crackers, crushed

1 cup sweetened flaked coconut

2 cups semi-sweet chocolate chips

1¼ cups (one 14-ounce can) sweetened condensed milk

2 cups pecans, lightly toasted (see Tip page 17) and coarsely chopped

- Preheat the oven to 350°F. Lightly butter a 9 x 13-inch pan and line with parchment paper, allowing enough overhang on the long side to lift the bars from the pan.

- Place the butter and graham crackers in a bowl and combine well. Transfer the mixture to the prepared pan and pat into an even layer to form the crust.

- Sprinkle the coconut evenly over the crust. Sprinkle the chocolate chips over the coconut. Pour the condensed milk evenly over the chocolate chips. Sprinkle the pecans evenly over the condensed milk layer. Press the layers down lightly. Transfer to the oven and bake until lightly browned, about 30 minutes.

- Set aside to cool completely and cut into 24 pieces.

lemon-pecan-coconut bars

YIELD: **2** DOZEN BARS

Reminiscent of pecan pie and lemon meringue, these sweet, tart, and salty bars have it all.

for the crust

1½ cups all-purpose flour

3 tablespoons granulated sugar

½ teaspoon kosher salt

1 stick (¼ pound) unsalted butter, chilled and cut into 8 slices

for the pecan filling

3 large eggs, at room temperature

1 cup light or dark brown sugar

1 cup pecans, lightly toasted (see Tip page 17) and chopped

¾ cup sweetened flaked coconut

1 teaspoon vanilla extract

for the lemon glaze

½ cup confectioners' sugar

¼ cup fresh lemon juice

2 teaspoons freshly grated lemon zest

- Preheat the oven to 350°F. Lightly butter a 9 x 13-inch pan and line with parchment paper, allowing enough overhang on the long side to lift the bars from the pan.

- **To make the crust:** Place the flour, sugar, and salt in the bowl of a mixer fitted with a paddle or a food processor fitted with a steel blade. Add the butter, a little at a time, and beat or pulse until the butter is completely incorporated. Press into the pan and pat into an even layer. Transfer to the oven and bake until golden, about 15 minutes. Set aside to cool completely.

- **To make the filling:** Combine all the ingredients in a mixing bowl and beat well. Pour over the cooled crust. Transfer to the oven and bake until just beginning to brown, 15 to 20 minutes.

- **To make the glaze:** Place all the ingredients in a bowl, whisk well, and brush over the still-warm filling.

- Set aside to cool completely, then cut into 24 pieces.

mmm...
lemony!

maida heatter's palm beach brownies with chocolate-covered mints
(slightly adapted)

These brilliantly designed, beyond-decadent, gorgeous, inspirational brownies are expensive and time-consuming to make but soooooooo well worth it. You'll find yourself making them again and again. They are absolutely amazing.

2 sticks (½ pound) unsalted butter

8 ounces unsweetened chocolate

5 large eggs, at room temperature

3¾ cups granulated sugar

2 teaspoons vanilla extract

¼ teaspoon kosher salt

1⅔ cups all-purpose flour

2 cups walnuts, lightly toasted (see Tip page 17) and chopped

Two 14- or 15.4-ounce bags York chocolate-covered peppermint patties, unwrapped

- Preheat the oven to 425°F. Line a 9 x 13-inch pan with aluminum foil, shiny side up. Use your hands to press down on the sides and corners of the foil to shape it to the pan. Lightly butter the foil.

- Place the butter and chocolate in a small saucepan over the lowest possible heat and cook, stirring, until almost all the chocolate has melted. Off heat, stir until smooth. Set aside to cool to room temperature.

- Place the eggs, sugar, vanilla, and salt in the bowl of a mixer fitted with a whisk attachment and whip on high speed for 10 minutes. Replace the whisk attachment with the paddle, lower the speed to low, and slowly add the chocolate mixture. Add the flour and beat on the lowest speed until just combined. Remove the bowl from the mixer and stir in the walnuts by hand.

- Pour half the mixture (about 3½ cups) into the prepared pan and smooth the top. Place a layer of the mints, touching each other and the edges of the pan, all over the chocolate layer. Cut some mints to fill in large spaces on the edges. (You will not use all the mints; there will be some left over.) Pour the remaining chocolate mixture over the mints and smooth the top.

- Transfer to the oven and bake for 15 minutes. Rotate the pan and bake an additional 20 minutes. The brownies should have a firm crust on top, but if you insert a toothpick in the center it will come out wet and covered with chocolate. It is done and you should not continue baking.

- Set aside to cool. Cover the pan with a cookie sheet and invert the pan and the sheet. Remove the pan and the foil lining. Cover the brownie with a length of waxed paper and another cookie sheet and invert again, leaving the brownie right side up.

- Refrigerate at least 4 hours and up to overnight. When you are ready to cut into brownies, use a long, heavy knife with a sharp blade either serrated or straight—try both. Cut into quarters. Cut each quarter in half, cutting through the long sides. Finally, cut each piece into 4 bars, cutting through the long sides. (These are better in narrow bar shapes than in squares.)

- Pack in an airtight box or wrap individually in clear cellophane, waxed paper, or foil. These freeze perfectly and can be served very cold or at room temperature.

BAKE SALE TIP ⅊ helium balloons

Helium balloons at bake sales always seem to draw a crowd. They don't cost a lot and are something children love as a souvenir. And they are yet another way to ask for a donation.

gooey chocolate chip sandwich bars

YIELD: 32 BARS

Think of the chocolate chip cookies as the bread and the chocolate and condensed milk as the filling, and you have gooey chocolate chip sandwich bars. Oh my, these are sinful. Don't cut them too big.

2 cups semi-sweet or white chocolate chips

One 14-ounce can sweetened condensed milk

2 teaspoons vanilla extract

1 batch cookie dough (pages 3, 5, and 25)

- Preheat the oven to 350°F. Lightly butter a 9 x 13-inch pan and line with parchment paper, allowing enough overhang on the long side to lift the bars from the pan.

- Place the chocolate chips and condensed milk in a small saucepan over the lowest possible heat and cook, stirring constantly, until the chocolate has melted and the mixture has thickened, 3 to 5 minutes. Off heat, add the vanilla and stir until smooth. Set aside to cool to room temperature.

- Using half the batch of cookie dough, place dollops on the prepared pan and press down lightly to even it out. Pour the cooled chocolate mixture over the dough and then add small dollops of the remaining dough to the top. Don't worry if the dollops don't completely cover the chocolate mixture.

- Transfer to the oven and bake until lightly browned, 20 to 25 minutes.

- Set aside to cool completely, then cut into 32 bars.

cream cheese brownies

The combination of the creamy smooth cheese and the rich brownies is absolutely scrumptious.

for the cream cheese layer

8 ounces (1 package) cream cheese, at room temperature

2 large egg yolks, at room temperature

¼ cup granulated sugar

2 tablespoons all-purpose flour

1 teaspoon vanilla extract

for the brownie layer

1 stick plus 2 tablespoons (10 tablespoons) unsalted butter

10 ounces semi- or bittersweet chocolate

4 large eggs, at room temperature

1½ cups granulated sugar

1 teaspoon vanilla extract

1 cup all-purpose flour

1 teaspoon baking powder

½ teaspoon kosher salt

1 cup semi-sweet chocolate chips (optional)

1 cup pecans or walnuts (optional), toasted (see Tip page 17) and coarsely chopped

- Preheat the oven to 325°F. Lightly butter a 9 x 13-inch pan and line with parchment paper, allowing enough overhang on the long side to lift up the brownies.

- **To make the cream cheese layer:** Place the cream cheese in the bowl of a mixer fitted with a paddle and beat until smooth. Add the egg yolk, sugar, flour, and vanilla, at a time, beating well after each addition. Scrape down the sides of the bowl, transfer to another bowl, and set aside. Clean the mixer.

- **To make the brownie layer:** Place the butter and chocolate in a small saucepan over the lowest possible heat and cook, stirring, until almost all the chocolate has melted. Off heat, stir until smooth. Set aside to cool to room temperature.

- Place the eggs and sugar in the bowl of a mixer fitted with a paddle and beat until lemon-colored and thick. Add the cooled chocolate mixture and vanilla and beat until well combined. Scrape down the sides of the bowl. Place the flour, baking powder, and salt in a separate bowl, mix well, and add to the chocolate mixture. If desired, add the chocolate chips and beat until well combined.

- Place half the chocolate mixture in the prepared pan, then dollop the cream cheese mixture over it and don't worry if the cream cheese doesn't cover the chocolate: it won't. Top with the remaining chocolate mixture. Take a table knife and gently draw it from east to west and then from north to south, making a checkerboard pattern. Do not allow the mixtures to combine too much. Sprinkle with the nuts, if desired.

- Transfer to the oven and bake until the sides, but not the top, are just beginning to brown, 25 to 30 minutes. Do not wait until a tester comes out clean: they will be overbaked at that point.

- Set aside to cool for about 10 minutes, then cut into 32 bars. Cover and refrigerate.

BAKE SALE TIP ❧ **keep it clean**

It's important to keep your bake sale clean and use proper hygiene. Hands touching food should be covered in gloves. Change gloves often, especially after handling any treats with nuts. Ask volunteers with long hair to pull it back or wear a hat. Have as many food items as possible covered with either glass, plastic wrap, or see-through plastic to keep any friendly insects from sampling the precious goods!

chocolate-crusted coconut-filled bars

YIELD: 32 BARS

The combination of chocolate, coconut, and walnuts makes these crunchy-and-chocolate-y on the bottom, gooey-and-rich on top brownies reminiscent of German Chocolate Cake. A bit time-consuming but worth every minute.

for the chocolate crust

2 ounces unsweetened chocolate, chopped

2 cups all-purpose flour

1 cup confectioners' sugar

½ teaspoon kosher salt

2 sticks (½ pound) unsalted butter, chilled and cut into small pieces

for the coconut filling

Two 14-ounce cans sweetened condensed milk

2 cups sweetened flaked coconut

1 cup walnuts or pecans, toasted (see Tip page 17) and lightly chopped

1 cup semi-sweet chocolate chips

- Preheat the oven to 350°F. Lightly butter a 9 x 13-inch pan and line with parchment paper, allowing enough overhang on the long side to lift up the bars.

- To make the chocolate crust: Place the chocolate in a small sauce-pan over the lowest possible heat and cook until almost all the chocolate has melted. Off heat, stir until smooth. Set aside to cool to room temperature but do not let it harden.

- Place the flour, sugar, and salt in a food processor fitted with a steel blade and process until combined. Add the butter, one chunk at a time, and process until it is pebbly. Add the cooled chocolate mixture and process until well combined. Pour into the prepared pan and transfer to the oven. Bake until just golden, 12 to 15 minutes. Set aside to cool.

- To make the coconut filling: Place the sweetened condensed milk, coconut, and walnuts in a bowl and mix well. Spread over the cooled crust, return to the oven, and bake until just golden, 20 to 25 minutes. Immediately sprinkle the chocolate chips over the filling, top with a tent of aluminum foil, and set aside until the chips melt, about 5 minutes. Remove the foil and using a table knife, spread the chips evenly across the top of the pan. Cool in the pan and cut into 32 bars.

BAKE SALE TIP ⁀ packaging

Bake sales aren't possible without delicious fresh-baked treats. But don't overlook the importance of pretty packaging for all those delicious baked goods. At Cookies for Kids' Cancer, we believe that a colorful bake sale table filled with well-packaged goodies will attract people and create a memorable experience.

Packaging musts include:
- Clear bags. Whether sealable, resealable, or needing ties/ribbons, using clear bags will allow supporters to see your yummy baked good.
- Craft bags with "windows." Because of Cookies for Kids' Cancer's distinctive craft-brown and green color scheme, using craft baggies is both efficient for offering baked goods by the half-dozen or dozen and they look adorable sitting on the table.
- Stickers. Cookies for Kids' Cancer stickers are available online in our Bake Sale Kits, along with an assortment of clear bags and donation jar signs.

fresh apple–cranberry bars

YIELD: 2 DOZEN BARS 🍃

If you're having a breakfast bake sale, do not forget these great morning bars. Feel free to substitute other fruits: we especially like the combination of pear and raisin.

for the filling

2 tablespoons unsalted butter

3 Granny Smith apples, cored, peeled, and cut into ½- to ¾-inch cubes

3 cups fresh or frozen cranberries

¾ cup granulated sugar

for the crust

2½ cups quick-cooking or old-fashioned rolled oats

2 cups all-purpose flour

1 cup light brown sugar

1 teaspoon ground cinnamon

1 teaspoon baking soda

2 sticks (½ pound) unsalted butter, melted

- Preheat the oven to 350°F. Lightly butter a 9 x 13-inch pan and line with parchment paper, allowing enough overhang on the long side to lift the bars from the pan.

- **To make the filling:** Place the butter in a large skillet over medium-high heat and when it has melted, add the apples, cranberries, and sugar. Cook, stirring, until the mixture has thickened and the liquid is syrupy, about 15 minutes. Set aside to cool completely.

- **To make the crust:** Place the oats, flour, sugar, cinnamon, baking soda, and butter in a bowl and toss to combine. Place half the mixture (1¾ to 2 cups) in the pan and pat down to make an even layer. Top evenly with the cranberry mixture, then top with the remaining oat mixture. Pat down lightly to make an even layer. Transfer to the oven and bake until the top is just beginning to brown, about 45 minutes. Set aside to cool to room temperature, then cover and refrigerate before cutting.

- Cut into 24 bars.

Kids' Cancer" labels for the water bottles. It was amazing—all of the kids stayed involved during the whole sale and were so proud. Very few people asked for change and some left donations and passed on all of the goods. The best part of the sale was the involvement that the kids had—they all were genuinely excited and happy to be helping kids who needed it. Our cousin's Girl Scout troop wants to know when they can have another bake sale!

Lesa Helbein, Charlotte, NC

I went to an event in honor of Grier Christenbury—a sweet, adorable, brown-eyed boy in my son's

Greg Aurigemma, Hasbrouck Heights, NJ

Our town sponsors a townwide garage sale. We figured this would be a great time to have the bake sale. My wife coordinated everything, contacted our neighbors, friends, and families, let them know of the upcoming sale, and asked them to bake for the sale. We had such a great response, with a table overlfowing with baked goods. We also had bottles of water, lemonade, and iced tea. We made posters and signs along with labels on all of the baked items, and we even made "Thank You for Supporting Cookies for

preschool class who was diagnosed with cancer at the age of two. Grier and his family were standing on a stage on one side of the lake with other pediatric cancer families who were waiting for their young cancer warriors to get medals for being so brave.

After the medals were distributed, the families on the other side of the lake released balloons for every child who lost their battle with cancer in our area. I looked over and thought about what it must be like for Grier's family watching those balloons go up and not knowing what side of the lake they may be on in years to come. It was heartbreaking to see and something shifted in me that very moment.

I also felt that parents who are battling cancer with their children shouldn't have to worry about raising funds to save their child's life. That afternoon I went to the Cookies for Kids' Cancer website and jumped right in—they made it so easy. One month later, we hosted our first team bake sale with two locations and raised almost $15,000. In addition to baked goods, we had cookie decorating, live music, a huge raffle, and a fire truck on hand that thrilled the kids. It was more than a bake sale—it was a chance for the community to come together to support Grier in the fight against this terrible disease.

Since then, we have coordinated six Cookies for Kids' Cancer events, raising over $100,000 in cash donations from individuals, a $50,000 donation from Bank of America, and matches from Glad through their Glad to Give program.

Even now, I'm amazed by our success. I was just a stay-at-home mom with a little extra time on my hands. It just goes to show that with a little determination anyone can raise a lot of dough for Cookies for Kids' Cancer. And we all should. After all, it's about kids.

The Theofiles Family,
Laurel, DE

Our inspiration is our son, Trace, who was diagnosed in 2008 with t-cell lymphoblastic lymphoma.

He inspires hundreds of people in our community. We held our bake sale at a restaurant. The day was extremely cold, but perfect for a holiday fundraiser for such a worthy cause. Unfortunately, our son Trace was unable to participate because he started running a fever the night before the sale. However, he helped sort, bag, and label the cookies a few days prior to the sale. We had over 100 volunteers who baked, bagged, and sold cookies. We feel so blessed to have had the privilege of helping out.

Denise Giaimo,
Piscataway, NJ

I have been searching for ways to put my education and fondness for baking to good use since my graduation. A single-screen movie theatre allowed us to have a bake sale/talent show in the theatre.

We contacted numerous friends with performance experience and asked them to participate in what was dubbed the Team Sweets Bake Sale & Talent Showcase. We created a website in order to put the official word out about the cause. The culmination of our efforts resulted in monetary donations and a feeling of goodness and warmth I had yet to experience in my own life. We procured nearly 1,000 baked goods. Coordinating this bake sale has easily been my most rewarding and satisfying accomplishment. We are honored to be a small part in the fight towards scientific discovery and the eradication of pediatric cancer.

cupcakes
FOR SALE

cupcakes and dessert cakes

mocha cupcakes with chocolate ganache and a coffee bean

YIELD: 18 STANDARD CUPCAKES OR 54 MINIS ⁊

Everyone loves a cupcake. These fabulous little bundles of decadence are a must at your bake sale. Not only do they taste incredible, cupcakes add interest and variety to the bake sale table. Display your cupcakes on cupcake stands or stack pretty platters to add height to your table.

We love to garnish these adult cupcakes with a whole coffee bean so they are easily distinguishable from chocolate cupcakes. You don't want a youngster running off with this coffee-laden treat.

1½ teaspoons coffee powder or ground espresso	½ teaspoon baking soda
½ cup hot water	¼ teaspoon kosher salt
½ cup plain low-fat (not nonfat) yogurt, sour cream, or whole milk	¼ teaspoon ground cinnamon
	1 stick (¼ pound) unsalted butter, at room temperature
1 teaspoon vanilla extract	1 cup granulated sugar
1⅓ cups all-purpose flour	1 large egg, at room temperature
½ cup unsweetened cocoa powder	Chocolate Ganache (page 83), for topping
1 teaspoon baking powder	Coffee beans, for garnish

- Preheat the oven to 375°F. Place paper liners in 18 cupcake/muffin tins. Alternatively, place paper liners in 54 mini muffin tins.

- Place the coffee powder and water in a small bowl and stir until the coffee has dissolved. Add the yogurt and vanilla and stir until well combined. Set aside.

- Place the flour, cocoa powder, baking powder, baking soda, salt, and cinnamon in a bowl and mix to combine.

- Place the butter and sugar in the bowl of a mixer fitted with a paddle and beat until light and fluffy, 3 to 5 minutes. Add the egg and beat well. Scrape down the sides of the bowl, add half the flour mixture and beat until combined. Add half the coffee mixture and beat until combined. Repeat with the remaining ingredients and beat well. Scrape down the sides of the bowl.

- Using a 2-ounce ice cream scoop or tablespoon, fill the prepared tins $2/3$ of the way.

- Transfer to the oven and bake until a toothpick inserted in the middle cupcake comes out clean, 22 to 25 minutes. Let cool in the pan for 5 minutes, then transfer cupcakes to a wire rack and set aside to cool.

- When fully cooled, top with Chocolate Ganache and garnish with a coffee bean!

BAKE SALE TIP location, location, location

Be sure to select a high-traffic location for your bake sale. Keep in mind where lots of people will be:
- Farmer's markets
- Festivals
- Parades
- Local coffee shops on a weekend morning
- Open-air shopping centers
- Outdoor concerts
- School athletic events
- Election Day polling sites
- Holiday events like Christmas parades or July 4th picnics

carrot cupcakes with maple cream cheese icing

YIELD: **2** DOZEN CUPCAKES

C arrots for breakfast? These are perfect, and your children won't even think they are eating vegetables!

for the cupcakes

1 cup canola oil

2 cups granulated sugar

4 large eggs, at room temperature

1 pound carrots, grated (about 4 cups)

1 cup pecans, walnuts, or hazelnuts (optional), toasted (see Tip page 17) and coarsely chopped

2 cups all-purpose flour

2 teaspoons baking soda

1 teaspoon kosher salt

1 teaspoon ground ginger

for the maple cream cheese icing

8 ounces (1 package) cream cheese, at room temperature

½ stick (2 ounces) unsalted butter, at room temperature

¾ cup confectioners' sugar

¼ cup maple syrup

- Preheat the oven to 350°F. Place paper liners in 24 cupcake/muffin tins.

- **To make the cake:** Place the oil, sugar, eggs, carrots, and pecans in a mixer fitted with a paddle and beat until well combined. Place the flour, baking soda, salt, and ginger in a separate bowl, mix well, and add to the sugar mixture. Mix until just combined. Scrape down the sides of the bowl.

- Using a 2-ounce ice cream scoop or heaping tablespoon, fill the prepared muffin tins ⅔ of the way. Transfer to the oven and bake until a tester comes out clean and the tops are slightly domed, 22 to 25 minutes. Let cool in the pan for 5 minutes, then transfer cupcakes to a wire rack and set aside to cool.

- **To make the icing:** Place all the ingredients in a mixer fitted with a paddle attachment or a food processor fitted with a steel blade and beat until smooth. When the cupcakes are completely cooled, generously spread the tops with icing. Refrigerate for at least 1 hour and up to overnight. Garnish with additional nuts, if desired.

BAKE SALE TIP ❧ *cupcake tips from melanie*

- Have all ingredients at room temperature.
- Don't overmix the batter or the cupcake will be tough and dry— just mix until it is completely incorporated and then STOP!
- Use cupcake liners! This makes cleanup easy and helps prevent the cupcakes from drying out.
- If cupcake batter is thick, put the batter in a pastry bag and pipe into cupcake pans. An alternative is to use an ice cream scoop.
- If cupcake batter is thin, ladle batter into a liquid measure and pour into cupcake pans.
- If you don't have cupcake pans, you can use 2 liners together and place on a cookie tray.
- Be careful not to overfill; ⅔ full is usually perfect.
- Check cupcakes about halfway into baking time—rotate the pan 90° to help ensure even baking.
- Don't overbake cupcakes. Cupcakes are ready when the surface is touched and the cupcake springs back. Or when you insert a toothpick in the center of a cupcake, the toothpick comes out clean or with crumbs, but not wet batter.
- Allow cupcakes to cool completely before decorating with frosting.
- Keep decorating simple—a quick swirl with a pastry bag or offset spatula. If it is hot weather, don't use buttercream for decorating! It will not hold up well at your bake sale.

---

lizzy's walnut butter cupcakes with chocolate ganache

YIELD: **2 DOZEN CUPCAKES** 🍂

Nutty and buttery, these cupcakes are a bit more sophisticated than the classic cupcake. Feel free to substitute pecans or almonds, and be sure to decorate the top with your nut of choice.

6 egg yolks, at room temperature

1 cup whole milk, divided

2¼ teaspoons vanilla extract

3 cups sifted cake flour

1½ cups granulated sugar

4 teaspoons baking powder

¾ teaspoon kosher salt

1½ sticks (6 ounces) unsalted butter, at room temperature

1 cup walnuts, lightly toasted (see Tip page 17) and chopped

Chocolate Ganache (page 83) for topping

- Preheat the oven to 350°F. Place paper liners in 24 cupcake/muffin tins.

- Place the egg yolks, ¼ cup milk, and vanilla in a small bowl and mix to combine.

- Place the flour, sugar, baking powder, and salt in the bowl of a mixer fitted with a paddle and mix to combine. Add the butter and remaining ¾ cup milk and beat on low speed until the dry ingredients are just moistened.

- Scrape down the sides of the bowl and beat on medium speed for 1½ minutes. Scrape down the sides again, then gradually add the egg mixture, and beat for 1 minute. Add the walnuts and stir.

- Using a 2-ounce ice cream scoop or a heaping tablespoon, divide the batter evenly between the prepared tins and transfer to the oven.

- Bake until a toothpick comes out clean, 25 to 35 minutes. Be sure not to overbake. Let cool in the pans for 5 minutes, then transfer cupcakes to a wire rack and set aside to cool.

- When fully cooled, top with Chocolate Ganache.

your basic, but fabulously rich, golden yellow cupcake with chocolate ganache

YIELD: **2** DOZEN CUPCAKES 〜

L et's face it: cupcakes are all about the decorations. They are the perfect canvas for add-ons: M and M's, sprinkles, chocolate chips, nuts, you name it.

Although these cupcakes are best when eaten the day they are made, we discovered that they store well if wrapped in plastic and left at room temperature up to 3 days.

3 cups all-purpose flour	2 large eggs, at room temperature
2 cups granulated sugar	
2 sticks (½ pound) unsalted butter, at room temperature	1 tablespoon vanilla extract
	1 tablespoon baking powder
1 cup sour cream	1 teaspoon kosher salt
4 large egg yolks, at room temperature	Chocolate Ganache (recipe follows)

- Preheat the oven to 350° F. Place paper liners in 24 cupcake/muffin tins.

- Place all the ingredients in a bowl and beat, by hand or with a mixer fitted with a paddle, until smooth and satiny. Scrape down the sides of the bowl and beat again.

- Using a 2-ounce ice cream scoop or a heaping tablespoon, divide the batter evenly between the prepared tins. Transfer the tins to the oven and bake until the tops are just beginning to color but not brown, 20 to 24 minutes. Let cool in the pan for 5 minutes, then transfer cupcakes to a wire rack and set aside to cool.

- Place 2 to 3 generous tablespoons ganache on each cooled cupcake and spread to smooth.

chocolate ganache

Make the ganache before you make the cupcakes. This ganache gets whipped and is therefore fluffy. If you want a denser frosting, simply omit the whipping stage. Feel free to substitute the semi-sweet chocolate with any other kind you like: bittersweet, milk, or white chocolate.

8 ounces semi-sweet chocolate, chopped or chips

1 cup heavy cream

- Place the chocolate in a medium-size heatproof bowl and set aside. Place the heavy cream in a small saucepan and cook over medium-high heat until it just comes to a boil, 3 to 4 minutes. Add the hot cream to the chocolate, then cover with a plate and set aside until the chocolate has melted, about 5 minutes. Stir until smooth, then cover and refrigerate until cooled, 45 minutes to 1 hour.

- Using a mixer fitted with a whisk attachment, whip the ganache until it is light brown and fluffy and forms medium-stiff peaks, about 2 minutes. Cover and set aside until ready to use.

BAKE SALE TIP ❧ **add color**

- Use bright ribbons on packaging.
- Make colorful stickers and labels.
- Don't forget the helium balloons.
- Encourage your volunteers to wear bright, inviting colors.

melanie karmazin's eggnog cupcakes

YIELD: **2** DOZEN CUPCAKES

Since you'll need store-bought eggnog for these adult-only cupcakes, be sure to keep an extra container in your fridge. On the other hand, if you love these as much as we do, you can buy eggnog when it is in season and freeze it in one-cup portions to defrost later.

3 cups all-purpose flour

1 teaspoon baking powder

½ teaspoon baking soda

2 sticks (1 cup) unsalted butter, at room temperature

2 cups granulated sugar

3 large eggs, at room temperature

1 cup eggnog

3 tablespoons bourbon

Eggnog Buttercream (recipe below) or whipped cream for topping

Freshly grated nutmeg

- Preheat the oven to 350°F. Place paper liners in 24 cupcake/muffin tins.

- Place the flour, baking powder, and baking soda in a bowl and mix well. Set aside.

- Place the butter and sugar in the bowl of a mixer fitted with a paddle and beat until light and fluffy, about 5 minutes. Add the eggs, one at a time, scraping down the sides of the bowl occasionally.

- Add one-third of the flour mixture to the egg mixture and beat. Add half the eggnog and beat. Beat in another third of the flour mixture and then beat in the remaining eggnog. Finish with the remaining dry ingredients. Stir in the bourbon. Scrape down the sides of the bowl.

- Using a 2-ounce ice cream scoop or a heaping tablespoon, fill the prepared tins. Transfer to the oven and bake until the cupcakes spring back when touched, 20 to 25 minutes. Let cool in the pan for 5 minutes, then transfer cupcakes to a wire rack and set aside to cool.

- Top with Eggnog Buttercream, or if you're having these at home, top with whipped cream and sprinkle with freshly grated nutmeg.

eggnog buttercream

4 large egg whites, at room temperature

1 cup granulated sugar

2 sticks (½ pound) unsalted butter, at room temperature and cut up into 1-inch pieces

4 tablespoons dark rum (optional)

1 teaspoon cinnamon (optional)

- Place the egg whites and sugar in the bowl of an electric mixer. Place the bowl over a double boiler and whisk constantly, by hand, until the mixture is just hot to the touch, 4 to 5 minutes. Carefully transfer the bowl to a stand mixer fitted with the whisk attachment and whisk until fluffy and cool to the touch, 4 to 5 minutes.

- Switch to the paddle attachment and add the butter, 2 tablespoons at a time, mixing until smooth. Add the rum and cinnamon, if using, and mix again until smooth. Cover and set aside until ready to use.

BAKE SALE TIP ❧ bring the community together

Bake sales bring everyone in the community together because who doesn't love a good cookie and a chance to give back? When planning your event, make sure to invite members of your local fire and police departments to stop by and have a cookie. Kids will be thrilled to see the firefighters pull up in the hook and ladder truck or police officers flash the lights in their cruisers. The men and women of these departments who serve the community every day often serve as heroes to kids, the same kids who you are raising money for who are our heroes.

---

coconut cupcakes with seven-minute frosting

YIELD: **2** DOZEN CUPCAKES

A coconut lover's dream come true, these cupcakes have the added richness and depth from coconut milk as well as the standard flaked coconut. We especially like these beauties (and they truly are) for spring, especially Easter, bake sales.

for the cupcakes

2 sticks (½ pound) unsalted butter, at room temperature

2 cups granulated sugar

3 large eggs, at room temperature

2 large egg yolks, at room temperature

3 cups all-purpose flour

1 tablespoon baking powder

¼ teaspoon kosher salt

1 cup canned unsweetened coconut milk, at room temperature, stirred well

2 teaspoons vanilla extract

1 cup sweetened flaked coconut

for the seven-minute frosting

2 large egg whites, at room temperature

¾ cup granulated sugar

3 tablespoons water

pinch cream of tartar

½ teaspoon vanilla extract

Pinch kosher salt

1 cup sweetened flaked coconut, for garnish

- Preheat the oven to 350°F. Place paper liners in 24 cupcake/muffin tins.

- **To make the cupcakes:** Place the butter and sugar in a mixer fitted with a paddle and beat until fluffy and lemon-colored, 3 to 5 minutes. Add the eggs and egg yolks, one at a time, beating well and scraping down the sides of the bowl after each addition.

- Place the flour, baking powder, and salt in a bowl and mix well. Add one third of the flour mixture to the butter mixture and beat well. Add ½ cup coconut milk and vanilla and beat well. Add another one third of the flour mixture and beat well. Add the remaining ½ cup coconut milk, beat well and then add the remaining flour mixture. Add the coconut and beat. Scrape down the sides of the bowl.

- Using a 2-ounce ice cream scoop or a heaping tablespoon, divide the batter evenly between the prepared tins and transfer to the oven. Bake until light golden and springy on top, 20 to 22 minutes. Let cool in the pan for 5 minutes, then transfer cupcakes to a wire rack and set aside to cool.

- **To make the seven-minute frosting:** Place the egg whites, sugar, water, and cream of tartar in the top of a double boiler over high heat. Beat with an electric mixer, egg beater, or whisk for 7 minutes (yes, this is really tiring). Off heat, add the vanilla and salt and continue beating until the frosting holds stiff peaks.

- Divide the frosting among the cooled cupcakes and garnish with a generous amount of additional coconut.

BAKE SALE TIP ⁊ **getting out the word**

It's important to get the word out about your event in the local media. Drop baked treats off at a local radio station during the morning drive-time to get local DJs talking about your event, contact the events section of your newspaper, send a notice to your local cable access channel, and contact the news department of TV stations. And don't forget the power of moms. Mommy bloggers and moms' groups are great resources for helping to spread the word about your event.

vermont maple cupcakes
with maple icing

YIELD: **18** CUPCAKES

I f you don't have real maple syrup, skip these cupcakes. Nothing else will do!

Wonderful for fall bake sales. You can also leave off the icing and serve these for breakfast!

for the cupcakes

2 cups all-purpose flour

1 tablespoon baking powder

¾ teaspoon kosher salt

1 cup real maple syrup

1 cup heavy whipping cream

2 large eggs, lightly beaten

1 stick (¼ pound) unsalted butter, melted and slightly cooled

for the maple icing

½ stick (4 tablespoons) unsalted butter, at room temperature

2 cups confectioners' sugar

⅓ cup real maple syrup

- Preheat the oven to 350°F. Place paper liners in 18 cupcake/muffin tins.

- **To make the cupcakes:** Place the flour, baking powder, and salt in the bowl of a mixer fitted with a paddle and stir to combine. Add the maple syrup, cream, and eggs, one at a time, beating well after each addition. Add the butter and beat until well combined. Scrape down the sides of the bowl.

- Using a 2-ounce ice cream scoop or a heaping tablespoon, fill the prepared muffin tins. Transfer to the oven and bake until a tester comes out clean, about 25 minutes. Do not allow the tops to get darker than a very light brown. Let cool in the pan for 5 minutes, then transfer cupcakes to a wire rack and set aside to cool.

- **To make the icing:** Place the butter, sugar, and maple syrup in the bowl of a mixer fitted with a paddle and beat until light and fluffy. Place 2 tablespoons on each cupcake and spread until smooth.

citrusy cupcakes with citrusy icing

YIELD: 2 DOZEN CUPCAKES 🐚

It's hard to decide if these are better solo orange, solo lemon, or a combination. Our suggestion: try it all three ways (though not at one bake sale) and decide for yourself. Be sure to decorate the icing with additional zest or, for those among you who are not purists, food coloring.

for the cupcakes

2 sticks (½ pound) unsalted butter, at room temperature

1¾ cups granulated sugar

3 large eggs, at room temperature

3 cups all-purpose flour

½ teaspoon baking soda

½ teaspoon kosher salt

1 cup buttermilk, plain low-fat yogurt, or sour cream

2 tablespoons freshly grated orange or lemon zest, or a combination

2 tablespoons fresh orange or lemon juice, or a combination

for the icing

2 cups confectioners' sugar

½ stick (2 ounces) unsalted butter, at room temperature

¼ cup fresh orange juice or 3 tablespoons lemon juice, or a combination

¼ cup fresh grated orange zest or 3 tablespoons lemon zest, or a combination (plus extra for garnish, optional)

- Preheat the oven to 350°F. Place paper liners in 24 cupcake/muffin tins.

- Place the butter and sugar in the bowl of a mixer fitted with a paddle and beat until light and fluffy, 3 to 5 minutes. Add the eggs, one at a time, and beat well. Add 1½ cups flour, baking soda, and salt and beat until combined. Add the buttermilk, orange zest, and orange juice and beat until combined. Add the remaining 1½ cups flour and beat well. Scrape down the sides of the bowl.

- Using a 2-ounce ice cream scoop or a heaping tablespoon, fill the prepared tins. Transfer to the oven and bake until a toothpick inserted in the middle comes out clean, about 20 minutes. Let cool in the pan for 5 minutes, then transfer cupcakes to a wire rack and set aside to cool.

- **To make the citrusy icing:** Place the confectioners' sugar and butter in a bowl and mix until creamy. Add the orange juice and orange zest and mix again. Cover and refrigerate until ready to use. Place 2 tablespoons on each cupcake and spread until smooth. Garnish with the extra zest, if desired.

BAKE SALE TIP ✦ packaging your cupcakes for the bake sale

- Cupcakes can be a little tricky to keep looking nice in transport or when displaying them at a bake sale. To keep your cupcakes clean and germ-free, either:
- Place each decorated cupcake in a 9-ounce clear plastic cup. You can then wrap plastic wrap around the cup from bottom to top and tie with a decorative ribbon. For a quick wrap, use Glad Press 'n' Seal over the top of the cup. Supporters will be able to see the cupcakes inside the cups, but no one can touch them.
- Or ask your local grocer to donate clear plastic cupcake boxes. Like individual cups, the boxes will allow people to see the pretty little cakes without touching or exposing them.

Pamela Hurtado, Galt, CA

My son's diagnosis of stage 4 liver cancer is what motivated us to become Good Cookies. When word spread about the bake sale, our community really stepped up to the plate to help this cause. We hope no child has to go through this tough journey.

Amanda Oliver, Raleigh, NC

Much like the ingredients for some of the world's best cookies, the ingredients for changing the world are pretty sweet and simple. A dash of love, a sprinkle of hope, stir in some determination, and bake until golden brown. Cancer does not know age, socioeconomic status, or race. I never want to take my health for granted, which is why it is so important for me to help children who deserve to be healthy. The world can become a safer and healthier place, one cookie at a time.

Sue Counsell, Granite City, IL

We set up in a three-sided tent to shield us from the cold. We offered drive-through service. People would pull up and tell us what they wanted, and we would deliver. We had a lot of help with the sale. After one of our leaders was on a radio station, we sold out in a little over an hour. It was very heartwarming to see the community support our efforts.

Harley Lower School, Rochester, NY

Our kids' wishes "that everyone can be healthy and strong" are our inspiration. On Martin Luther King, Jr. Day, our students do service projects for their community and raise money for charities that help kids and their families. Projects were tailored from the hopes and dreams of the kids. There was a cookie/ lemonade sale. Everyone's small change added up to make a big difference!

Erin K. Hodal, Long Grove, IL

Our organization, Mothers4Others, promotes volunteerism. By creating an avenue for women (mostly moms) and their supporters to reach out by donating time, goods and services, we support organizations that rely on community aid. We hosted a Cookies for Kids' Cancer bake sale, and all the proceeds from the evening were donated. We met so many wonderful people during the sale, who were all so giving!

Lauren Fitzgerald, Staten Island, NY

As a teacher, I was looking all over for great ideas to help my students learn about money, an especially hard concept to teach. Ideas that have the kids working with real money always hit the mark. Sometimes it is just as important to teach kids just how lucky they are. For example, at the holiday time, they do chores to raise money for a charity, I thought the bake sale would not only help them develop money smarts but teach them about community and that there are others who are less fortunate.

melanie karmazin's gingerbread cupcakes with cream cheese icing

YIELD: **20** CUPCAKES

F orget about making gingerbread houses: these cupcakes are easier
and far more delicious. Be sure to include them in fall bake sales!

2¼ cups all-purpose flour	¾ cup molasses
1 tablespoon ground ginger	¾ cup light brown sugar
1½ teaspoons ground cinnamon	3 large eggs
1½ teaspoons ground cloves	¾ cup buttermilk
¾ teaspoon baking soda	Cream Cheese Icing (recipe follows)
1½ sticks (6 ounces) unsalted butter, at room temperature	

- Preheat the oven to 350°F. Place paper liners in 20 cupcake/muffin tins.

- Place the flour, ginger, cinnamon, cloves, and baking soda in a bowl and mix well. Set aside.

- Place the butter, molasses, and sugar in the bowl of a mixer fitted with a paddle and beat until light and fluffy, 5 minutes. Add the eggs, one at a time, and beat well after each addition. Add one third of the dry ingredients and beat, then add half of the buttermilk and beat. Continue alternating dry with wet, finishing with dry. Scrape down the sides of the bowl

- Using a 2-ounce ice cream scoop or a heaping tablespoon, fill the prepared tins. Transfer to the oven and bake until the cupcakes spring back when touched, 20 to 25 minutes. Let cool in the pan for 5 minutes, then transfer cupcakes to a wire rack and set aside to cool.

- Place 2 tablespoons icing on each cupcake and spread until smooth.

cream cheese icing

1 stick (¼ pound) unsalted butter, at room temperature

1½ pounds (24 ounces or 3 packages) cream cheese, at room temperature

2 cups confectioners' sugar

1 tablespoon plus 1 teaspoon vanilla extract

- Place the butter and cream cheese in a bowl fitted with a paddle and beat until light and fluffy, 5 minutes. Add the sugar and vanilla and beat until smooth. Cover and refrigerate until ready to use.

BAKE SALE HOST TIP *from tisha soladay*

- Pick a high-traffic location.
- Brownies sell well. Top them with lots of good stuff like sprinkles, non pareils, crushed peppermint, or icing.
- Offer packages of three, six, or even twelve treats per bag or box.
- Have plenty of little bags for people to package their picks.

chocolate babka cupcakes

YIELD: **2** DOZEN CUPCAKES

Originally a wonderful cake chock-full of chocolate chips, walnuts, and cinnamon—definitely a bit rich for breakfast and yet definitely breakfast-y (or maybe best for afternoon tea). We experimented with babka as cupcakes and decided we like it this way even better than the original.

for the cupcakes

2 sticks (½ pound) unsalted butter, at room temperature

2 cups all-purpose flour

1½ cups light brown sugar

1½ cups sour cream or whole-milk yogurt

⅔ cup unsweetened cocoa powder

3 large eggs, at room temperature

1 tablespoon vanilla extract

1½ teaspoons baking powder

1 teaspoon baking soda

½ teaspoon kosher salt

for the streusel topping

1 cup semi-sweet chocolate chips, finely chopped

1 cup walnuts, lightly toasted (see Tip page 17) and finely chopped

3 tablespoons granulated sugar

1 teaspoon ground cinnamon

Pinch kosher salt

- Preheat the oven to 350°F. Place paper liners in 24 cupcake/muffin tins.

- **To make the cupcakes:** Place all the cupcake ingredients in a bowl and beat, by hand or with a mixer fitted with a paddle, until smooth and satiny. Scrape down the sides of the bowl and beat again.

- **To make the streusel:** Place all the streusel ingredients in a small bowl and stir to mix.

- Using a 2-ounce ice cream scoop or a heaping tablespoon, divide half the batter evenly between the prepared tins. Sprinkle with half the streusel topping and then top with the remaining batter. Sprinkle with the remaining streusel topping. Transfer the tins to the oven and bake until the tops are just beginning to color but not brown, 20 to 24 minutes. Let cool in the pans for 5 minutes, then transfer cupcakes to a wire rack and set aside to cool.

FOOD FOR THOUGHT ॐ nuts, no nuts, and other allergies . . .

The topic of allergies comes up all the time, and there is no bigger concern than whether or not to use nuts in bake sale treats. We have absolute respect and concern for individuals with nut allergies, as we know exactly how dangerous exposure can be. While it is tempting to shy away from recipes that contain nuts out of consideration for those with allergies, the reality is individuals with severe allergies would be advised to avoid eating anything homemade at a bake sale. The simple absence of nuts from a recipe does not mean the ingredients and baking equipment are nut-free. There is almost no way to avoid cross-contamination at home or even in an industrial bakery.

Another common question involves offering gluten-free and dairy-free baked goods. Not only do we encourage offering at least one gluten-free option, we've found amazing local bakery partners willing to donate gluten-free or dairy-free products to events, when asked with plenty of notice.

cocoa-carrot cupcakes with white chocolate chips

adapted from the mansion on turtle creek cookbook by dean fearing

YIELD: 2 DOZEN CUPCAKES

Don't turn up your nose at this strange-sounding combination—carrots, cocoa, and white chocolate is actually a brilliant union.

2 cups light brown sugar	2 teaspoons baking soda
1½ cups canola oil	¼ teaspoon kosher salt
4 large eggs, at room temperature	1 pound carrots, grated (about 4 cups)
1¾ cups all-purpose flour	2 cups white chocolate chips
5 tablespoons unsweetened cocoa powder	

- Preheat the oven to 350°F. Place paper liners in 24 cupcake/muffin tins.

- Place the sugar, oil, and eggs in a mixer fitted with a paddle and beat until well combined. Place the flour, cocoa powder, baking soda, and salt in a separate bowl and mix well. Add to the oil mixture, scrape down the sides of the bowl, add the carrots and chocolate chips, and mix again. Scrape down the sides of the bowl.

- Using a 2-ounce ice cream scoop or heaping tablespoon, fill the prepared tins. Transfer to the oven and bake until a tester comes out clean and the tops are slightly domed, 22 to 25 minutes. Let cool in the pan for 5 minutes, then transfer cupcakes to a wire rack and set aside to cool.

black cocoa cupcakes

YIELD: **20** CUPCAKES 🐦

A bit like Devil's Food Cake, these cupcakes are so intense, they glisten.

2 cups granulated sugar	1 cup prepared coffee
1¾ cups all-purpose flour	½ cup canola oil
¾ cups unsweetened cocoa powder	2 large eggs, at room temperature
2 teaspoons baking soda	1 teaspoon vanilla extract
1 teaspoon baking powder	Confectioners' sugar, for dusting
½ teaspoon kosher salt	
1 cup sour cream or whole-milk yogurt	

- Preheat the oven to 350°F. Place paper liners in 20 cupcake/muffin tins.

- Place the sugar, flour, cocoa powder, baking soda, baking powder, and salt in a bowl and mix to combine. Set aside.

- Place the remaining ingredients except the confectioners' sugar, in a mixer fitted with a paddle and beat until everything is incorporated. With the mixer on low speed, slowly add the dry ingredients and beat until shiny, about 4 minutes. Scrape down the sides of the bowl.

- Using a 2-ounce ice cream scoop or heaping tablespoon, fill the prepared tins. Transfer to the oven and bake until a tester comes out clean and the tops are slightly domed, 22 to 25 minutes. Let cool in the pan for 5 minutes, then transfer cupcakes to a wire rack and set aside to cool. When fully cooled, dust with confectioners' sugar.

sour cream–poppy seed babycakes

YIELD: 2 DOZEN BABYCAKES ﭏ

If you love poppy seeds, you'll flip for these fabulous babycakes. Perfect for bake sales, these are best made 2 to 3 days ahead of time to let sit well-wrapped for optimal flavor.

1 cup whole milk	1⅓ cups granulated sugar
¾ cup poppy seeds	3 large eggs, at room temperature
½ cup sour cream or whole-milk yogurt	2 cups all-purpose flour
2 tablespoons fresh lemon juice	1 tablespoon baking powder
1 tablespoon vanilla extract	½ teaspoon kosher salt
2 sticks (½ pound) unsalted butter, at room temperature	

- Preheat the oven to 350°F. Place paper liners in 24 cupcake/muffin tins.

- Place the milk and poppy seeds in a small saucepan and bring to a low boil over medium-high heat. Set aside to cool for 15 minutes, then add the sour cream, lemon juice, and vanilla and beat well. Set aside.

- Place the butter and sugar in the bowl of a mixer fitted with a paddle and beat until light and fluffy, 3 to 5 minutes. Add the eggs, one at time, beating well after each addition. Add 1 cup flour and beat well. Scrape down the sides of the bowl and add half the reserved poppy seed mixture, continuing to beat.

- Scrape down the sides of the bowl, add the baking powder, salt, and the remaining 1 cup flour and beat well. Scrape down the sides of the bowl, add the remaining poppy seed mixture, and beat well. Scrape down the sides of the bowl.

- Using a 2-ounce ice cream scoop or a heaping tablespoon, fill the prepared tins. Transfer to the oven and bake until the babycakes spring back when touched, 20 to 25 minutes. Let cool in the pan for 5 minutes, then transfer babycakes to a wire rack and set aside to cool.

cardamom babycakes

YIELD: **2** DOZEN BABYCAKES ⅗

W e've taken the classic rich, rich, rich sour cream coffeecake and put it into cupcakes to make a modern-day babycake. Even so, it takes willpower to eat just one!

for the babycakes

2 sticks (½ pound) unsalted butter, at room temperature

2 cups light brown sugar

2 large eggs, at room temperature

2 cups all-purpose flour

2 cups sour cream or whole-milk yogurt

1 to 2 teaspoons ground cardamom

½ teaspoon baking powder

¼ teaspoon kosher salt

2 teaspoons vanilla extract

for the streusel

1 cup walnuts, lightly toasted (see Tip page 17) and finely chopped

⅓ cup brown sugar

2 teaspoons ground cinnamon

- Preheat the oven to 350°F. Place paper liners in 24 cupcake/muffin tins.

- **To make the babycakes:** Place all the babycake ingredients in a bowl and beat, by hand or with a mixer fitted with a paddle, until smooth and satiny. Scrape down the sides of the bowl and beat again.

- **To make the streusel:** Place the streusel ingredients in a small bowl and mix well.

- Using a 2-ounce ice cream scoop or heaping tablespoon, divide half the batter evenly between the cupcake tins. Sprinkle with half of the streusel topping and then top with the remaining half of the batter. Sprinkle with the remaining streusel topping. Transfer the tins to the oven and bake until the tops are just beginning to color but not brown, 20 to 22 minutes. Let cool in the pan for 5 minutes, then transfer babycakes to a wire rack and set aside to cool.

paige retus' banana bread/muffins

YIELD: 2 LOAVES OR 2 DOZEN MUFFINS

You really can't have a bake sale without including Paige's famous banana bread. We don't know why, but in spite of including all the same ingredients, her recipe is better than any other.

7 to 8 overripe bananas ("the nastier the better," says Paige)

2 cups granulated sugar

2 sticks (½ pound) unsalted butter, melted and slightly cooled

4 large eggs, at room temperature

2 teaspoons vanilla extract

2 cups all-purpose flour

1 cup whole wheat graham flour

1 tablespoon baking soda

1 teaspoon kosher salt

1 cup walnuts (optional), lightly toasted (see Tip page 17) and chopped

- Preheat the oven to 350°F. Lightly butter 2 standard-size loaf pans or place paper liners in 24 cupcake/muffin tins.

- Place the bananas and sugar in the bowl of a mixer fitted with a paddle and beat 5 minutes. Add the butter, eggs, and vanilla, beating well and scraping down the sides of the bowl after each addition. Scrape down the sides of the bowl; add the flours, baking soda, salt, and stir in the nuts, if using, until combined.

- Pour into the prepared pans, or using a 2-ounce ice cream scoop or heaping tablespoon, fill the prepared tins. Transfer to the oven and bake until golden brown and firm in the center, about 1 hour for the breads and 20 to 25 minutes for the muffins. Let cool in the pan for 5 minutes, then transfer to a wire rack and set aside to cool.

Wendy Martin, Richmond, VA

Anyone who has ever faced pediatric cancer will tell you that—despite being an abhorrent coward—it's a powerful opponent. Medical professionals use surgeries and toxic treatments to fight it. Friends and families use hope, love, and prayer (among other things).

But imagine if could redirect cancer's own rage and power right back at it? This, I realized, is exactly what Cookies for Kids' Cancer does.

One day Cookies for Kids' Cancer founder Gretchen Holt-Witt posted this status update to her Facebook page: "It wasn't good news. It was awful news. We start high-dose chemo on Monday morning. My heart is literally

shattering into a million pieces. But I'll pick myself up and go at it again. Liam needs me. He needs all of us. Pray for him and hold a bake sale."

Those words were read 300 miles away in Richmond, Va. And just 20 days later—in direct response to cancer's attack—a handful of bake sale coordinators, a dozen "team captains," and hundreds of moms, dads, caring souls, big-hearted businesses, kids, scouts, and students raised more than $34,000 to fund desperately needed pediatric cancer research. Every dollar earned was matched by a grant from The Glad Products Company.

The Richmond sale was unbelievably inspirational for everyone involved. Several mothers approached our team captains asking, "How can my family get involved in something like this?" One woman bought a pile of cookies. After listening to our sales pitch on the need for better treatments she said, with tears in her eyes, "I know... I'm a nurse in a pediatric cancer ward."

A young college student expressed her delight at our cause, explaining that she was a pediatric cancer survivor. A Hispanic man on a bicycle gazed at an image of one of the children battling cancer and handed over a crumpled bill. When a volunteer encouraged him to take a bag of cookies, he shook his head and said, in broken English, "I just want to help." As he rode away, she unfolded the bill and discovered it was a twenty. Her Facebook status at the end of that day said what we all felt: "What I know for sure is that people want to help, they just need to be given a way to."

Robyn Chirichella, Holmdel, NJ

I am also a cancer survivor and it absolutely breaks my heart when I see children suffer from cancer. I spoke to my principal about involving the entire school.

My class made posters and advertised to the whole school for five days leading up to the bake sale. On the day of the bake sale the entire fourth grade class came to school, armed with their cookies and baked goods to sell, sell, sell their hearts out with huge smiles and encouraging words. It was amazing to see the love the children had for this sale, and for the campaign. The "cookie elves" were all over the school selling their cookies. Children came to school emptying their piggy banks, and others used money they had been saving. Kids were handing twenty-dollar bills and just buying one or two cookies. One little boy said to me, "Mrs. Chirichella, here is twenty dollars because I never want to see another boy or girl hurting from this disease." My lunch aide donated fifty dollars: "children should never suffer," she whispered in my ear. It was amazing to see the whole school come and support this bake sale! We reflected on how proud we were of each other. When you open your heart and help others, nothing but wonderful things can and will always happen.

applesauce bread/muffins

YIELD: **2** LOAVES OR **2** DOZEN MUFFINS

We love this recipe because they are delicious and wonderfully moist, but also because it's easy to have all the ingredients on hand. These are perfect for breakfast bake sales as well as for those held later in the day.

4 large eggs, at room temperature

1½ cups granulated sugar

3 cups applesauce, at room temperature

2 sticks (½ pound) unsalted butter, melted and slightly cooled

3 cups all-purpose flour

1 tablespoon baking soda

1 teaspoon kosher salt

½ teaspoon ground cinnamon

2 cups walnuts (optional), lightly toasted (see Tip page 17) and chopped

- Preheat the oven to 350°F. Lightly butter 2 standard-size loaf pans or place paper liners in 24 cupcake/muffin tins.

- Place the eggs and sugar in the bowl of a mixer fitted with a paddle and beat until lemon-colored and thickened, 2 to 3 minutes.

- Add the applesauce and butter, beating well and scraping down the sides of the bowl before each addition. (The mixture will break, and while you may think you've ruined it, just keep on going, everything is fine. It just looks sort of gritty.) Place the flour, baking soda, salt, and cinnamon in a separate bowl and mix well. Add to the applesauce mixture and beat to combine. Add the nuts, if desired, and mix well. Scrape down the sides of the bowl.

- Pour into the prepared pans, or using a 2-ounce ice cream scoop or heaping tablespoon, fill the prepared tins. Transfer to the oven and bake until golden brown and firm in the center, about 1 hour for the breads and 20 to 25 minutes for the cupcakes. Let cool in the pan for 5 minutes, then transfer to a wire rack and set aside to cool.

green zucchini bread

We'd never suggest sneaking vegetables into food to fool your kids, and yet, if they like this bread—which is very similar to carrot cake—it might make them realize that zucchini is actually very tasty!

6 large eggs, at room temperature	½ teaspoon baking powder
2 cups light brown sugar	2 teaspoons kosher salt
2 cups canola oil	2 teaspoons ground cinnamon
2 cups all-purpose flour	4 cups grated zucchini
2 cups graham flour	2 teaspoons vanilla extract
1 tablespoon plus 1 teaspoon baking soda	2 cups walnuts (optional), lightly toasted (see Tip page 17) and chopped

- Preheat the oven to 350°F. Lightly butter 2 standard-size loaf pans or place paper liners in 24 cupcake/muffin tins.

- Place the eggs and sugar in the bowl of a mixer fitted with a paddle and beat until lemon-colored and thickened, about 2 to 3 minutes. Add the remaining ingredients except for the nuts and beat well. Reserve about ¼ cup of the nuts, if using. Stir in the remaining nuts, if using, by hand. Scrape down the sides of the bowl.

- Pour into the prepared pans, or using a 2-ounce ice cream scoop or heaping tablespoon, fill the prepared tins. Sprinkle the reserved nuts, if using, on top. Transfer to the oven and bake until a tester comes out clean, about 1 hour for the breads and 20 to 25 minutes for the muffins. Let cool in the pan for 5 minutes, then transfer to a wire rack and set aside to cool.

baby grainy irish soda breads

YIELD: 2 DOZEN BREADS

W e've substituted some of the traditional white flour with whole wheat graham flour, cornmeal, wheat germ, and flax seed to make a more grainy, more interesting version of Irish soda bread. It's been so popular we recently had an eight-year-old boy practically beg for the recipe!

2 cups all-purpose flour

1 cup whole wheat graham flour

½ cup yellow cornmeal

¼ cup toasted wheat germ

¼ cup ground flax seed

1 tablespoon baking powder

2 teaspoons kosher salt

2 teaspoons granulated sugar

1 teaspoon baking soda

1½ sticks (6 ounces) unsalted butter, chilled or frozen, cut into thin slices

2 large eggs

1½ cups sour cream, plain low- or full-fat yogurt, or buttermilk

1 cup currants (optional)

1 large egg yolk, beaten

- Preheat the oven to 375°F. Line a baking sheet with parchment paper.

- Place the flours, cornmeal, wheat germ, flax seed, baking powder, salt, sugar, and baking soda in the bowl of a food processor fitted with a steel blade and process until combined. While the processor is going, add the butter, a few slices at a time, and process until the mixture resembles cornmeal.

- Place the eggs and sour cream in a large mixing bowl and mix well. Add the flour mixture and currants, if using, and beat, by hand with a spoon, until combined. Form into 24 balls, place on the prepared pan and using your palm, flatten down a bit. Using the tip of a sharp knife, make an X in the tops and then brush with the egg yolk. Transfer to the oven and bake until the bottom sounds hollow when tapped and the top is golden brown, about 20 minutes. Let cool on the pan for 5 minutes, then transfer to a wire rack to cool.

emily's pumpkin-chocolate chip muffins

YIELD: 3 DOZEN MUFFINS

Emily's six- and three-year-old sons know it's fall when she starts making these muffins. Not only do they love the muffins themselves, they love the experience of baking with her.

This recipe is perfect for your fall events because one recipe makes so many muffins. They are sturdy, flavorful, appealing to kids, and hit the spot anytime of the day. Emily often bakes a double batch of muffins—one for a bake sale and one to have on hand for the kids.

One 16-ounce can pumpkin puree	2 teaspoons baking soda
4 large eggs, at room temperature	2 teaspoons baking powder
1½ cups granulated sugar	2 teaspoons ground cinnamon
1 cup canola oil (or half applesauce, half oil)	1 teaspoon salt
3 cups all-purpose flour	2 cups semi-sweet chocolate chips

- Preheat the oven to 400°F. Place paper liners in 36 cupcake/muffin tins (alternatively, use 8 dozen mini-muffin tins).

- Place the pumpkin, eggs, sugar, and oil in the bowl of a mixer fitted with a paddle and beat until thickened, about 2 to 3 minutes.

- Place the flour, baking soda, baking powder, cinnamon, and salt in a separate bowl, mix well, and add to the pumpkin mixture. Add the chocolate chips and beat to combine. Scrape down the sides of the bowl.

- Using a 2-ounce ice cream scoop or heaping tablespoon, fill the prepared tins. Transfer to the oven and bake until brown, 16 to 20 minutes. Let cool in the pan for 5 minutes, then transfer to a wire rack and set aside to cool.

morning glory muffins

YIELD: 2 DOZEN MUFFINS

These fabulous muffins debuted at The Morning Glory Café on Nantucket Island and the name stuck. A little bit carrot cake, a little bit apple muffin, these muffins are the rare treat that don't suffer from the absence of some of its star ingredients, in this case, pineapple, raisins, pecans, and coconut.

3 large eggs, at room temperature

1 cup canola oil

1 teaspoon vanilla extract

2¼ cups unbleached all-purpose flour

2 cups grated carrots

1 cup granulated sugar

1 cup (8 ounces) canned crushed pineapple, drained well

¾ cup raisins, currants or dried cranberries

½ cup pecans or walnuts, lightly toasted (see Tip page 17) and coarsely chopped

½ cup sweetened flaked coconut

1 apple, peeled and grated

1 tablespoon ground cinnamon

2 teaspoons baking soda

½ teaspoon salt

- Preheat the oven to 350°F. Place paper liners in 24 cupcake/muffin tins.

- Place the eggs, oil, and vanilla in a bowl and using a whisk, mix until fluffy. Add the remaining ingredients and stir well. Scrape down the sides of the bowl.

- Using a 2-ounce ice cream scoop or heaping tablespoon, fill the prepared tins. Transfer to the oven and bake until the tops are golden brown and a tester comes out clean, 20 to 25 minutes. Let cool in the pan for 5 minutes, then transfer to a wire rack and set aside to cool.

citrusy corn muffins

citrusy corn muffins

YIELD: 2 DOZEN MUFFINS

Morning bake-sale goers will love this citrus-packed version of cornbread. If you don't have all the citrus fruits on hand, don't worry: as long as you end up with 2 tablespoons citrus zest, you can use just one or two of them.

2 cups all-purpose flour

1 cup yellow cornmeal

1½ teaspoons baking powder

1 teaspoon baking soda

½ teaspoon kosher salt

2 large eggs, at room temperature

¾ cup granulated sugar

1 tablespoon freshly grated orange zest

2 teaspoons freshly grated lemon zest

1 teaspoon freshly grated lime zest

1 stick (¼ pound) unsalted butter, melted and slightly cooled

¾ cup sour cream or whole-milk yogurt

½ cup whole milk

- Preheat the oven to 400°F. Place paper liners in 24 cupcake/muffin tins.

- Place flour, cornmeal, baking powder, baking soda, and salt in medium bowl and mix to combine. Set aside.

- Place eggs, sugar, and orange, lemon, and lime zest in a bowl and mix until thick, about 1 minute. Slowly add butter, whisking constantly. Slowly whisk in the sour cream and milk and whisk to combine. Add egg mixture to flour mixture and mix until just combined. Do not overbeat. Scrape down the sides of the bowl.

- Using a 2-ounce ice cream scoop or heaping tablespoon, fill the prepared tins. Transfer to the oven and bake until the tops are golden brown and a tester comes out clean, 20 to 25 minutes. Let cool in the pan for 5 minutes, then transfer to a wire rack and set aside to cool.

Glenn Austin Bliss,
Great Falls, MT

I was inspired to have a charity event by the upper-classmen at my school who were doing fundraisers. After hearing about Cookies for Kids' Cancer, I knew I wanted to host a bake sale. My mom gave me the idea of asking the owner of our local minor league baseball stadium if I could have a bake sale at a game. He said yes and, with my mom's help, I decided that 200 dozen cookies and a goal of $2,000 would be appropriate. Our next step was getting the word out.

First, I spoke at a non-profit organization to promote the bake sale, which is where the local media learned about the fundraiser. The speech led to a TV interview. The TV interview led to an article in the paper. Soon, news about my fundraiser was viral around the community. When the word was spread and more people heard about it, I received a lot of phone calls from people who wanted to bake and volunteer. Many businesses agreed to sponsor the bake sale with donations directly to Cookies for Kids' Cancer. I received a phone call from a girl who offered to help sell cookies. I would never have guessed she has a little brother with rare form of cancer called alveolar rhabdomyosarcoma. She helped me realize my bake sale was about more than just raising money—my bake sale brought people together in the fight against pediatric cancer.

By the time the last dollar was donated, the bake sale raised almost $20,000—nearly ten times our original goal. We were so excited that everyone who came to the bake sale wanted to help as much as we did.

Misty Wallace, Winona, MO

I am the Children's Church Leader at my church. Our last teaching unit was titled "Kids Can." I was looking for a service project that my kids could do. A Cookies for Kids' Cancer bake sale was perfect! We held our bake sale during our church's fellowship dinner. People donated sugar cookies, icing, and toppings. The kids did all the decorating themselves. There were close to 20 kids involved from ages three to nine. They had a great time and were proud to be helping other kids.

Kendel Lively, Daleville, VA

The students and faculty of Lord Botetourt High School held a school-wide bake sale on Pediatric Cancer Awareness Day. Students wore hats for a dollar donation and the entire school was given gold ribbons to wear. We also sold candy and held a bake sale to make "the letter C stand for cookies" and candy instead of cancer. The event was a success. We are committed to making a difference one cookie at a time.

raisin bran–wheat germ muffins

Don't even consider having a morning bake sale without these earthy treats.

3 cups all-purpose flour

2 cups wheat or oat bran

1 cup wheat germ

1 teaspoon ground cinnamon

1 teaspoon kosher salt

2 sticks (½ pound) unsalted butter, at room temperature

⅔ cup granulated sugar

4 large eggs, at room temperature

1 cup sour cream

1 cup yogurt

⅔ cup molasses

2 teaspoons vanilla extract

2 cups raisins, currants, or dried cranberries

- Preheat the oven to 350°F. Place paper liners in 24 cupcake/muffin tins.

- Place the flour, bran, wheat germ, cinnamon, and salt in a bowl and mix well. Set aside.

- Place the butter and sugar in the bowl of a mixer fitted with a paddle and beat until smooth, 2 to 3 minutes. Add the eggs, one at a time, beating after each addition. Add the sour cream, yogurt, molasses, and vanilla and beat until smooth. Gradually add the flour mixture and beat just until incorporated. Add the raisins. Scrape down the sides of the bowl.

- Using a 2-ounce ice cream scoop or a heaping tablespoon, fill the prepared tins. Transfer to the oven and bake until a tester comes out clean, 20 to 25 minutes. Let cool in the pan for 5 minutes, then transfer to a wire rack and set aside to cool.

apricot-almond scones

S cones are not often found at bake sales, but we don't know why: they are perfect for anyone who doesn't want something sweet and they hold up incredibly well. Feel free to substitute both the nuts and dried fruit for any combination that suits you.

2⅔ cups all-purpose flour

½ cup brown sugar

1 tablespoon baking powder

1 teaspoon kosher salt

1½ sticks (6 ounces) unsalted butter, chilled and cut into slices

1 cup almonds, lightly toasted (see Tip page 17) and coarsely chopped

1 cup coarsely chopped dried apricots

½ cup low-fat or whole-milk yogurt

2 large eggs, at room temperature

- Preheat the oven to 375°F. Line 2 baking sheets with parchment paper.

- Place the flour, sugar, baking powder, and salt in the bowl of a mixer fitted with a paddle and mix to combine. Gradually, while the mixer is running, add the butter, and pulse until the mixture resembles coarse cornmeal. Remove the bowl from the mixer, add the remaining ingredients, and mix by hand until the dough just comes together. Do not overmix.

- Divide the dough into 20 slightly flattened balls and place on the prepared baking sheets. Transfer to the oven and bake until they are golden, about 25 minutes. Let cool on the pans for 5 minutes, then transfer to a wire rack and set aside to cool.

parmesan scones

A great alternative for people who don't want sweets, these savory, cheesy scones work well at both morning and afternoon bake sales.

3 cups all-purpose flour

¼ cups granulated sugar

1 tablespoon baking powder

1 teaspoon kosher salt

1½ sticks (6 ounces) unsalted butter, chilled and cut into slices

1 cup freshly grated Parmesan cheese

½ cup low-fat or whole-milk yogurt

4 large eggs, at room temperature

- Preheat the oven to 375°F. Line 2 baking sheets with parchment paper.

- Place the flour, sugar, baking powder, and salt in the bowl of a mixer fitted with a paddle and mix to combine. Gradually, while the mixer is running, add the butter, and pulse until the mixture resembles coarse cornmeal. Remove the bowl from the mixer, add the remaining ingredients, and mix by hand until the dough just comes together. Do not overmix.

- Divide the dough into 20 slightly flattened balls and place on the prepared baking sheets. Transfer to the oven and bake until they are golden, about 25 minutes. Let cool on the pan for 5 minutes, then transfer to a wire rack and set aside to cool.

Say cheese!

cheese
BITES

parmesan cheese bites

YIELD: ABOUT 2 DOZEN BITES

A great option for something savory instead of sweet, these fabulous little savory snacks are not just for bake sales; we also love to serve these at dinner parties.

1 cup all-purpose flour

⅔ cup freshly grated Parmesan cheese

¼ teaspoon cayenne pepper

1 stick (¼ pound) unsalted butter, cut up into tiny bits

2 tablespoons whole milk

- Place the flour, cheese, cayenne, and butter in a food processor and pulse until well blended.
- Shape the dough into 2 logs, wrap in plastic wrap, and place in an airtight container. Refrigerate at least 8 hours and up to 2 days.
- Preheat the oven to 350°F. Line a baking sheet with parchment paper.
- Remove the dough from the wrapping, cut into ¼-inch slices, and transfer to the prepared baking sheet. Brush each slice with milk and bake until golden brown, 12 to 14 minutes. Set aside to cool.

BAKE SALE TIP 🐦 set a goal

Fundraisers that have a financial goal give people a purpose. Share your goal with signage at your event like a drawing of a donation jar or a sketch of a glass of milk that can be marked indicating how close you are to your goal.

BAKE SALE TIP 🦢 host a bake sale in the morning

- Promote your bake sale as a "Breakfast Bake Sale." Encourage guests to go "out" for breakfast the day of your event. Send out a "Save the Date" email to remind friends and community members about your event.
- Arrange to have coffee and juice in addition to baked goods.
- Feature muffins, breads, scones, and a few cookies like our Oatmeal Raisin Cranberry Cookies (page 5).
- Color-coordinate your décor for the season—plates, napkins, forks, and cups can all reflect the season or holiday.
- Raffle off breakfast-related items—travel mugs or a set of coffee mugs; gift cards to local coffee shops; gift certificates for brunch at a local restaurant; or a waffle iron or pancake griddle from a local cooking store. Most businesses are happy to donate goods or services—all you need to do is ask!
- Remind everyone that 100% of the funds they donate will go directly to Cookies for Kids's Cancer.

lucques brown scones

YIELD: **2 DOZEN SCONES** 𝒷⁓

Adapted from the famous Lucques restaurant in Los Angeles, these breakfast and afternoon scones are perfect for anyone looking for something substantial but not sweet.

2¼ cups all-purpose flour

¾ cup whole-wheat flour

3 tablespoons granulated sugar

2 tablespoons plus 2 teaspoons baking powder

1 teaspoon kosher salt

9 tablespoons unsalted butter, chilled and cut into small cubes

1 cup plus 2 tablespoons buttermilk

- Preheat the oven to 375°F. Lightly butter a baking sheet.

- Place the flours, sugar, baking powder, and salt in a food processor fitted with a steel blade and process 30 seconds, until well combined.

- Add the butter and pulse about 10 times, until the mixture resembles coarse cornmeal.

- With the machine running, quickly pour in 1 cup of the buttermilk. Stop the machine as soon as the dough comes together. It's important not to overwork the dough.

- Turn the dough onto a lightly floured work surface and form it together with your hands into a large ball. Divide the dough into three pieces, and shape each of them into a 5-inch-wide disc. Cut each disc into quarters.

- Brush the tops of the scones with a little buttermilk. Place on the prepared baking sheet and bake 25 minutes, until the scones are golden brown. Transfer to racks to cool.

BAKE SALE TIP ⁀ pricing

The question we hear most often: "How much should I charge per item?" Our answer—don't set a price at all. Simply offer your treats in exchange for a donation.

The whole idea behind Cookies for Kids' Cancer is to raise funds for research and to raise awareness of the needs surrounding the number one disease killer of children in the U.S. Money raised at bake sales will be used to fund new and improved treatments for all types of pediatric cancer. With this in mind, if you do not set prices or set graduated suggested donation levels ($5—Good Cookie Giver, $10—Huge Cookie Heart, $20—Captain of the Cookie Kingdom), you have the opportunity to talk to each person who comes to the bake sale about why you are raising money and the importance of every dollar donated. When people learn the difference their donation will make in the fight against pediatric cancer, they often go back to their wallet or purse to give more.

Thank every person who donates, no matter what they give, for their gift and encourage them to get involved by hosting their own Cookies for Kids' Cancer bake sale.

crunchy, candy-like, and salty stuff

chocolate-covered caramel-laced matzo

YIELD: ABOUT **16** SERVINGS

Though not typical bake sale fare, these have an amazing combination of textures and flavors, and once you try them you will be hooked. Since it's almost impossible to cut these into uniform sizes, we like to either weigh or eyeball these and sell them in little bags.

4 to 5 pieces of matzo

1 stick (4 ounces) unsalted butter

½ cup light brown sugar

1 teaspoon vanilla extract

1¼ cup bitter or semi-sweet chocolate chips

1 cup sliced almonds, lightly toasted (see Tip page 17) and chopped

½ teaspoon kosher or sea salt

- Preheat the oven to 350°F. Line a baking sheet with foil, allowing a little bit of overhang on the long sides.

- Line the baking sheet with the matzo, being careful not to overlap matzo.

- Place the butter and sugar in a small heavy saucepan and bring to boil over medium-high heat. Continue cooking, stirring constantly, until the bubbles have bubbles, 2 to 3 minutes. Do not let it burn. Off heat, carefully add the vanilla and mix well. Drizzle the mixture over the matzo and using a pastry brush or metal spatula, spread the mixture evenly.

- Transfer to the oven and bake just until it is bubbling and starts to look dry, 10 to 12 minutes. It can burn easily, so be careful. Remove from oven and sprinkle with the chocolate chips, and return to the oven for 1 minute. Let stand until the chocolate is almost all melted, about 5 minutes, then spread chocolate evenly over the top.

- Sprinkle with the almonds and salt. Set aside in a cool area or refrigerate until the chocolate has set up. Break into pieces.

crunchy, candy-like, and salty stuff 137

maple pecans

YIELD: 4 CUPS 🍂

Another great item to offer, these slightly spicy, slightly sweet, definitely crunchy, addictive pecans are a great bake sale alternative to baked goods.

1 large egg white,
at room temperature

4 cups pecans, lightly toasted
(see Tip page 17)

½ cup real maple syrup

2 tablespoons unsalted butter,
melted

½ teaspoon kosher salt

¼ teaspoon cayenne pepper

¼ teaspoon black pepper

- Preheat the oven to 225°F. Line 2 baking sheets with parchment paper.

- Place the egg white in a large stainless steel bowl and whisk until frothy.

- Place the remaining ingredients in a large bowl and mix well. Add the egg whites and toss until well coated. Transfer to the prepared sheets and arrange in a single layer. Place in the oven and bake until golden brown, about 30 minutes. Immediately loosen the nuts with a spatula and set aside to cool.

Mandy Schroeder, Carrier, OK

I am 15 years old. A second grader at my school was diagnosed with leukemia. These bake sales were a part of my food and nutrition and citizenship projects in 4-H. I am thankful that this worthy organization exists, so I could be a part of helping.

Mrs. Patti Lidtke and Mrs. Maria Smith, Fifth-Grade Teachers, Sarasota, FL

Our fifth grade at St. Martha Catholic School embraced Catholic Schools Week theme, "Celebrate Service," and chose to have a bake sale. Our fifth graders did all the advertising, sales, setup, and cleanup. They set up a sale table each day during the morning break. The fifth grade is proud of what we raised, thanks to the generosity and support of the parents, grandparents, teachers, staff, and students in our school community.

Dana Jo Valleyjo, Clewiston, FL

I became involved with Cookies for Kids' Cancer because children are our future. We held a bake sale the Wednesday before Thanksgiving. We offered whole pies and cakes since we knew people would want them for their Thanksgiving dinner. I decided to have it at our local family restaurant. During our bake sale a woman who fought and beat cancer came into the restaurant to donate cash because she was happy to know that someone was trying to raise funds for pediatric cancer. When the bake sale should have been over, we were not ready to give up. Instead we took our jumbo bell outside in the rain and started ringing it for people to see our bake sale. We raised just over $500 with four girls and a table full of cookies, pies, breads, and cakes. But that wasn't enough. During this bake sale we were talking about what we could do for Christmas. We decided on a presale for pies. We limited ourselves to selling just four types of pies. With 75 presale orders, we used four ovens and one whole day to bake. We raised almost $500 this time. It doesn't matter how much help you have or how much money you raise. Whether it's $100

or $1,000, every dollar counts. You make a difference to help the children of our future.

Lori Scott, Imperial, MO

We had two locations, and 21 wonderful people baked goods for our sale. We had ten varieties of cookies, as well as full cakes and pies, homemade granola, and the list goes on. It's a wonderful feeling to see people give during these tough economic times. I had no idea what to expect! I certainly feel grateful for all my friends and family and blessed that we can contribute to a good cause.

crunchy, candy-like, and salty stuff 141

pine nut brittle

Although this nut brittle is good any time of year, it's especially nice if you enjoy giving something unusual for a homemade holiday gift.

Do not even think about making this unless you have a candy thermometer; it's critical.

3 cups granulated sugar

1 cup Lyles Golden Syrup (you can substitute corn syrup)

¼ cup (2 ounces) unsalted butter

¼ cup water

2 teaspoons vanilla extract

5 cups pine nuts, lightly toasted (see Tip page 17)

- Line 2 baking sheets with parchment paper. Lightly butter a metal offset spatula.

- Place the sugar, syrup, butter, water, and vanilla in a medium-size saucepan and cook over medium-high until it reaches a boil. Lower the heat to low and cook, stirring constantly, until the temperature reaches the soft-crack stage, about 275°F on the candy thermometer, 10 to 12 minutes.

- Quickly add the pine nuts and immediately pour the mixture onto the prepared sheets. Using the spatula, spread the brittle as thinly as possible. Relax; after 30 seconds there is no more influencing the mixture. Set aside to cool completely. Break into large pieces. Store in an airtight container.

white chocolate and pistachio bark

YIELD: ABOUT 12 PIECES

The combination of white chocolate, dried cranberries, and pistachios has become a classic, but the variations on bark are endless. Substitute the white chocolate with dark or milk chocolate; the cranberries for raisins, apricots, or dates; and the pistachios for any gourmet nuts, including lightly salted pecans, walnuts, cashews, or Virginia peanuts. Put the bark in little bags.

1 pound white chocolate

1 cup dried cranberries

2 cups shelled pistachios, lightly toasted (see Tip page 17)

- Line a baking sheet with parchment paper.
- Place the chocolate in the top of a double boiler and cook over medium heat until it melts. Set aside to cool for 5 minutes. Pour onto the prepared cookie sheet and sprinkle with the cranberries and pistachios. Cover and refrigerate at least 1 hour and up to overnight. Break into pieces.

BAKE SALE HOST TIP *from christine ray-cook*

- Packs of three cookies in seasonal/festive cellophane bags with ribbons sell well. Chocolate chip cookies and cupcakes always sell. I have done a few bake sales, and cupcakes made with buttercream frosting, neatly frosted with a piping bag, sell.
- To transport your treats to your event, use large disposable containers with lids.
- Presentation is key, and having kids around during the bake sale adds fun and joy to the event.

chex mixes

C hex cereals are gluten-free and therefore a great offering to those with celiac disease. You can have bags of fun colors, textures, and shapes for your supporters to sample. The mixes can be as simple as Chex cereals, nuts, dried fruits, and mini chocolate chips. Be creative. They can be made several days ahead and are ready when you are.

2 cups Corn Chex

2 cups Rice Chex

⅔ cup Wheat Chex

20 thin pretzel sticks, broken in half

½ cup pecans, walnuts, almonds, or peanuts, lightly toasted (see Tip page 17)

½ cup raisins, currants, or chopped dried apricots

2 teaspoons canola oil

- Preheat the oven to 250°F. Lightly oil a baking sheet.
- Place everything in a bowl and toss well. Pour the mixture onto the baking sheet and bake until lightly golden, about 15 minutes. Set aside to cool and then divide into bags of 1 cup each.

chocolate-covered pretzels

Pretzel rods will add color and variety to your table. Be sure to package them in clear bags to show them off and to keep little hands from grabbing one and taking a bite.

Pretzel rods can be dipped in chocolate, butterscotch, white chocolate, or a combination. They are easy to prepare and can be decorated in such fun ways. We break the rods in half, then dip the broken ends into melted chocolate. Tap off the excess chocolate and roll in chopped nuts, crushed peppermint candies, or rainbow sprinkles. Let rods dry on cooling rack until they are set. You can also drizzle pretzel rods with another color chocolate to create a zebra effect. The rods are beautiful when bundled in groups of 3 to 5 and placed in a clear cellophane bag and tied with a ribbon or raffia. Pretzel rods fly off our table during our bake sale.

BAKE SALE TIP ⌇ **weather**

Seasons and weather impact a bake sale in many ways. While everyone hopes for sunny, mild weather, be prepared for worst-case scenarios based on the season. We've had bake sales in blizzards, heat waves, and day-long rains. When it comes to cupcakes, be sure to have a back-up plan for keeping them cool in the summertime, since seeing melted icing on a cupcake is unappealing. If selling cupcakes during summer, keep them in the shade, under an event tent, or even in a portable cooler on ice.

Calabasas High School, Calabasas, CA

I know a flu shot may help prevent the flu, but I never thought getting a flu shot would inspire me to host a bake sale that could save lives. Let me explain.

I was sitting in the doctor's office waiting to get a flu shot when I came across a magazine article about Gretchen Holt-Witt and her son Liam who was diagnosed with cancer at the age of two. The article described how she decided to fight back for her son Liam and for all kids fighting cancer and started a charity to help raise money for childhood cancer research through bake sales. At that moment I realized that a Cookies for Kids' Cancer bake sale was something I could and wanted to do with my family.

My kids were excited about the idea. They passed out letters and sent emails to their friends to help. My husband and I rallied our friends and family to bake cookies. We had no idea what to expect at that 1st bake sale, but we were overwhelmed with the amount of generosity and support from our community. Weeks later, people kept asking us when our next bake sale was and how they could help. That's when my son had the idea of starting a club at his high school called the Calabasas High School Cookies For Kids' Cancer Club. After the 1st club rush he had a list of over 100 students who wanted to join the club. After just three bake sales, they've raised thousands of dollars and inspired the community to support their effort.

I'm so proud of all the students and the work they do for this charity. As Gretchen's story inspired me, these students inspire others to make a difference.

Angie Collins, San Marcos, CA

My Junior Girl Scout Troop held a bake sale at the Annual Christmas Tree-Lighting Ceremony. We always donate a portion of our fund-raising proceeds to charity. There are so many parallels with our troop. Bake sale, cookies, kids! The girls were very touched to help further research for pediatric cancers.

Jennifer Dixon, Scotch Plains, NJ

Rather than individual service projects, our "Student Movement Against Cancer" Club held a bake sale during lunches over a week. Over 30 students were involved in the planning, selling, and

promoting of the bake sale. So many of our students have been personally affected by cancer, whether it's a sibling, a parent, or grandparent. We hope that our contribution will continue to show the dedication of many in the fight against pediatric cancer.

Leslie Stern Abramowitz, Port Washington, NY

Each Hebrew school class has to complete a "Mitzvah Project" of their choice. A classmate and friend has been struggling with leukemia. The fourth-grade class made its choice clear: we want to help fight pediatric cancer. The kids felt a sense of accomplishment making the posters and selling the cookies (we also sold ices since it was a hot day). We hope we helped the cause.

index